Stanislav Grof

Books of the Dead

Manuals for Living and Dying

with 148 illustrations, 16 in colour

Thames and Hudson

ART AND IMAGINATION

British Library Cataloguing-in-Publication Data

A Catalogue record for this book is available from the
British Library

ISBN 0–500–81041–9

Printed and bound in Singapore by C.S. Graphics

Contents

The Ancient Books of the Dead

One of the major tolls modern humanity has had to pay for the rapid technological development following the scientific and industrial revolutions is a progressive alienation from its biological nature and loss of connection with the spiritual source. During the period of rapid evolution of materialistic science and precipitous technological progress, three basic areas that link humans to nature – birth, sex, and death – were subjected to deep psychological repression and denial. At the same time, the spiritual awareness that had provided a sense of meaningful belonging to the cosmos was replaced by atheism, or superficial religious activities of decreasing vitality and relevance.

At the beginning of this century, depth psychology inspired by the studies of Sigmund Freud initiated a sexual revolution that has greatly increased our understanding of instinctual life and radically transformed cultural attitudes and behaviour. Interest in non-ordinary states of consciousness, triggered by psychedelic research and widespread self-experimentation in the 1960s, has attracted attention to the problems related to birth and death. This resulted in the study of the psychological impact of the birth trauma, development of pre- and perinatal psychology, and the introduction of new obstetric practices. Systematic study of non-ordinary states of consciousness together with the pioneering work with patients suffering from incurable diseases conducted by Dr Kübler-Ross and others then led to an unprecedented renaissance of interest in the psychology of dying and near-death experiences.

It is not easy to understand why the public suddenly became open to issues related to death. Even at the time of the deepest cultural denial there were isolated researchers, particularly parapsychologists, who were studying various aspects of death and dying and publishing papers and books on their findings. Special publications, such as Jess E. Weisse's *The Vestibule*, Jean-Baptiste Delacour's *Glimpses of the Beyond*, or Karlis Osis's *Death-Bed Observations of Physicians and Nurses*, described and discussed strange experiences reported by people who had come close to death and lived to tell their stories. For some reason, the professional circles and the general public paid very little attention to these reports until Raymond Moody's *Life After Life* became overnight an international best-seller.

Moody's book was a study of near-death experiences based on interviews with 150 individuals who had had a close brush with death. Rather than making a breathtaking new discovery, Moody basically confirmed the findings of many of his predecessors. He showed that people who come close to death experience a series of most extraordinary adventures in consciousness that deserve serious attention of professionals as well as laymen. As Moody himself pointed out, similar experiences had been reported not only in earlier decades, but throughout centuries. The literature of ancient cultures, who had a remarkably sharp awareness of the spiritual and philosophical importance of death, abounds in eschatological passages.

The ancient texts that are specifically dedicated to the problems of death and dying are usually referred to as 'books of the dead'. The oldest of these texts is the so-called Egyptian Book of the Dead; it is a collection of ancient Egyptian papyri based on a body of literature called *Pert em hru*, usually translated as Manifestation in the Light, or Coming Forth By Day. Probably the most famous of these documents is the Tibetan Book of the Dead, known under the name *Bardo Thödol*, or Liberation by Hearing on the Afterdeath Plane. Mesoamerican examples are the Maya Book of the Dead, which can be reconstructed from the pictures and texts on the funeral vases of the so-called Ceramic Codex, and comparable Toltec and Aztec material from the preserved screenfold codices. To these can be added a range of medieval European eschatological material known as *Ars moriendi – The Art of Dying*.

When the ancient 'books of the dead' first came to the attention of western scholars they were considered to be fictitious accounts of the posthumous journey of the soul, and as such, wishful fabrications of people who were unable to accept the grim reality of death. They were put in the same category as fairy tales – creations of human fantasy of undoubted beauty, but no relevance for everyday reality. However, a deeper study of these texts revealed that they had been used as guides in the context of sacred mysteries and spiritual practice, and very likely described the experiences of the initiates and practitioners. From this new perspective, presenting the books of the dead as manuals for the dying may be seen as a clever disguise to obscure their secret ritual function and protect their esoteric message from the uninitiated.

Modern research focusing on non-ordinary states of consciousness brought unexpected new insights into this problem area. Systematic study of the experiences in psychedelic sessions, powerful non-drug forms of psychotherapy, and spontaneously occurring psychospiritual crises, showed that in all these situations, people can encounter an entire spectrum of unusual experiences, including sequences of agony and dying, passing through hell, facing divine judgment, being reborn, reaching the celestial realms, and confronting memories from previous incarnations.

These states are strikingly similar to those described in the eschatological texts of ancient and pre-industrial cultures. Such experiences seem to originate in the collective unconscious as described by C.G. Jung, and their specific symbolism can be drawn from many different cultures of the world, not necessarily the subject's own. Moreover, thanatological studies of near-death states showed that the experiences associated with life-threatening situations bear deep resemblance to the descriptions from the ancient books of the dead, as well as to those reported by subjects in psychedelic sessions and modern experiential psychotherapy. It has become clear that these texts are actually maps of the inner territories of the psyche encountered in profound non-ordinary states of consciousness.

It is possible to spend one's entire lifetime without ever experiencing these realms, or even being aware of their existence, until one is catapulted into them at the time of biological death. However, for some people this experiential area opens up during their lifetime in a variety of situations, including psychedelic sessions or other powerful forms of self-exploration, serious spiritual practice, participation in shamanic rituals, or during spontaneous psychospiritual crises. This offers us the possibility of experiential exploration of these territories of the psyche on our own terms, before it is imposed on us by biological death.

The experiential practice of dying, or 'dying before dying', has two important consequences. It liberates the individual from the fear of death and changes his or her attitude toward dying, and so prepares him or her for the experiences at the time of biological demise, and by eliminating the fear of death, it transforms the individual's way of being in the world. For this reason, there is no fundamental difference between the preparation for death by exploration of dying, on the one hand, and spiritual practice leading to enlightenment, on the other. This is the reason why the ancient books of the dead could be used in both situations.

Thanks to the findings of modern consciousness research amassed during the last few decades, we can attempt in this book to do more than just present the actual historical material of the books of the dead, and review the information amassed by scholars who have subjected these texts to expert professional analysis. We can compare this information with the observations from thanatology and other areas of modern consciousness research, such as psychedelic studies, experiential psychotherapy, anthropology, comparative religion and mythology, and show the relevance of these ancient texts for contemporary readers.

Manifestation in the Light: The Egyptian Book of the Dead

One of the most famous funerary texts is the so called Egyptian Book of the Dead, or *Pert em hru*. The English name is misleading, since it suggests a comprehensive and coherent work associated with a specific author, or at least with a definite historical period. In actuality, *Pert em hru* is a vast and heterogeneous collection of texts, some of which are spells and incantations, prayers, hymns, litanies and magical formulae, others mythological sequences, or procedures for treating the deceased. These texts originated in different historical eras, and in their totality they span a period of almost five millennia.

The title Egyptian Book of the Dead is derived from the name given by Egyptian tomb-robbers to every roll of inscribed papyrus they found with mummies – *Kitab al-Mayitun*, or 'book of the dead person'. The original Egyptian title *Pert em hru* is usually translated as 'manifestation in the light', 'coming forth by day', or 'chapters of everyday arrival'. From this large body of funerary texts, the ancient scribes made specific selections for the benefit of a particular individual, brought them together in a comprehensive way, and provided them with rich illustrations. Instead of a standard and uniform text, we thus have many individualized and unique collections that bear the names of the deceased, such the papyri of Ani, Hunefer, or Anhai, now in the British Museum in London.

The funerary texts were originally written only for kings, and were inscribed on the walls of certain pyramids, such as those erected in the honour of the pharaohs Cheops, Chephren and Mykerinos in Sakkara. Both the pyramids and the pharaohs for whom they were built were related to the sun god, Ra. These so-called 'Pyramid Texts' were produced between 2350 and 2175 BC, and are among the oldest written records, not only in Egypt, but in the whole of human history. However, the material they contain points to sources that are even more archaic. The preoccupation with afterlife and belief in the beyond that led to the practice of mummification is known in Egypt from about 3100 BC.

After about 1700 BC, the practice of burial with funerary texts was extended from the pharaohs to members of the nobility and other prominent figures. The so-called 'Coffin Texts' took the form of scrolls, or were painted on the sides of wooden coffins. The most famous of these funerary texts came from the city of Thebes, like the papyri of Ani, Hunefer and Anhai, mentioned above. One of the principal figures of *Pert em hru*, the sun god Ra, was the state deity of Thebes.

From the first to the last, the texts of *Pert em hru* reveal the unalterable belief of the Egyptians in the immortality of the soul, resurrection, and life after death. However, the message of these texts is not consistent and coherent like that of their Tibetan counterpart, the *Bardo Thödol*. From the oldest to the youngest, the Eygptian funerary texts span a period of almost five thousand years. Even a conservative culture such as ancient Egypt undergoes significant changes in the course of millennia. In addition, various cities had their preferences in regard to principal deities, and there were differences, conflicts, and power struggles between the priests of Heliopolis, Memphis, Thebes, and Hermopholis. New deities were adopted and often worshipped alongside the old.

In spite of the great complexity of the funerary texts, one can discern two major ideological streams. On the one hand, great emphasis was put on the sun god Ra, his divine retinue, and their archetypal nocturnal-diurnal journey. In the mythology underlying this belief, the sun god accompanied by his crew of assisting deities travelled in a splendid solar boat. In the daytime, they proceeded in a large arc across the Egyptian sky. Toward the end of the day, at sunset, the barge disappeared in the opening in mountains of the West and entered the underworld, Tuat, a dismal and terrifying region full of treacherous places, demons and other dangerous creatures. This 'unseen place' contained abysmal depths of darkness and firepits in which the damned, the enemies of Ra, were consumed. The sun god and his retinue had to overcome daily all the challenges of this ominous realm.

Those who worshipped Ra as their principal deity believed that after physical death they would join him and his crew and travel with them in the solar barge. Their principal text was *Am Tuat*, or 'The Book of What is in the Tuat', written by the priests of Amen-Ra to proclaim the sun god's supremacy. The *Am Tuat* provided for the followers of Amen-Ra the information about the divisions of the Tuat, the knowledge of the Halls and Gates and the names of the beings who guarded them, and the necessary magic formulae and power-words for the safe passage of the solar barge and its crew.

On the other hand, an older tradition of the ancient mortuary god Osiris also permeated the texts of *Pert em hru*. Osiris, one of four divine siblings, was killed and dismembered by his evil brother Seth, and the parts of his body were dispersed all over the Nile delta. Reassembled and resurrected by his two divine sisters, Isis and Nephthys, he became the god and ruler of the Egyptian underworld. His followers expected to join him after death in Sekhet Hetepet, or Happy Fields, a paradisean replica of the Nile Valley, and enjoy eternal life cruising on the celestial river, worshipping deities, feasting on exquisite food, and engaging in joyful agricultural activities.

The principal text of the followers of Osiris was the Book of the Gates; it was compiled to prove that, despite the pretensions of the priests of Amen-Ra, the ancient god of the dead, Osiris, was still the overlord of the underworld and that his kingdom was everlasting. This text, the most complete version of which was found inscribed on the alabaster sarcophagus of Pharaoh Seti I (around 1375 BC), consisted of two parts. The first is a series of texts and pictures which describe the progress of the sun god to the kingdom of Osiris, the Judgment of the Dead, the life of the beatified in Sekhet Hetepet, and the punishment of the wicked and the foes

The god Ra in the solar barque. The deity changes his form according to the stage of the journey

The funeral procession of Ani, c. 1250 BC, is shown in his papyrus of the Book of the Dead. It illustrates Chapter I, with words to be spoken on the day of burial, when the deities Thoth, Horus, Ra and Orisis are invoked for the journey into the underworld and the 'coming forth by day' of the sun god and Osiris. The second part consists of a series of texts and pictures which represent the magical ceremonies that were performed in very ancient times to reconstruct the body of the sun god and make him rise every day.

The story of the death and rebirth of Osiris played such an important role in Egyptian eschatological mythology that it deserves to be briefly told. The four divine siblings Isis, Osiris, Nephthys and Seth were the children of Geb, the god of the earth, and Nut, the goddess of the sky. Osiris was also the husband of his sister Isis, and Nephthys the wife of her brother Seth. According to the legend, Osiris was an enlightened king who civilized the Egyptians, taught them the art of agriculture, and prohibited cannibalism. His brother Seth hated him, and with his fellow-conspirators plotted his death.

Seth invited Osiris to a banquet where he showed him a richly decorated chest made specially for him, and invited him to try it. Once Osiris lay inside, Seth slammed the lid and secured it with nails. The chest was thrown into the river Nile and floated down to the sea. It drifted to Byblos, on the Phoenician coast, where it came to rest on the shore, and a lovely tree grew up and enclosed it. The tree's size and beauty captured the attention of Malacander, the King of Byblos, who had it cut down to be used as a pillar of his palace.

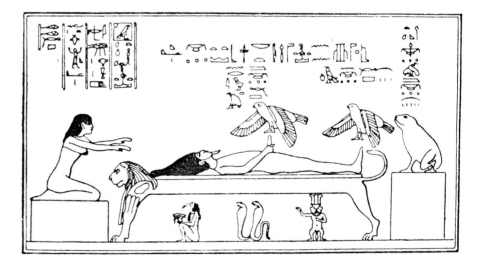

Isis in the form of a kite, begetting Horus by the dead Osiris, and (below) Anubis reconstituting the body of Osiris, directed by the god Thoth and helped by the frog goddess Heqet. (After bas reliefs at Philae)

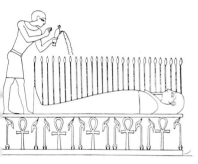

Isis nursing her son Horus, concealed in the papyrus swamps, and attended by Thoth and Amen-Ra. *Below*: Corn grows from the body of the dead Osiris. Inscribed beneath is the *ankh*, symbol of eternal life, framed by the characters for 'good fortune' and 'wellbeing'. (After bas reliefs at Philae)

Isis, as sister, lover and wife to Osiris, searched for him everywhere, weeping, while the land of Egypt dried up and the vegetation withered. Isis finally discovered the pillar in the palace in Byblos, and succeeded in obtaining it from the queen after serving for some time as a nurse to the little prince. She returned on a ship to Egypt with Osiris's body, and on the way, managed to conceive a child by perching upon Osiris in the form of a kite. Fearing that Seth could discover Osiris's body and her pregnancy, she hid in the marshes. Seth had not given up his plan to destroy Osiris. Hunting in the marshes, he came upon the body, hacked it into fourteen pieces, and scattered them to the four winds.

Isis and Nephthys, with the help of the jackal-headed deity Anubis, found and gathered all the pieces together in a rawhide and succeeded in resurrecting Osiris, who then became the Lord of the Underworld. Horus, Isis's child by the dead Osiris, grew up to become the avenger of his father. After a long and hard struggle, he defeated Seth and castrated him. The death and resurrection of Osiris was for the Egyptians an important archetypal pattern for survival after death. The battle between Horus and Seth became a metaphor for the cosmic battle between the forces of light and darkness, or good and evil.

In the mystical tradition of Egypt, the experience of death and rebirth was not necessarily bound to the time of the biological demise. The sacred temple mysteries of Isis and Osiris gave neophytes the opportunity to confront death long before old age or disease made it mandatory, and to conquer it and discover their own immortality. In initiatory procedures of this kind, neophytes not only lost the fear of death, but also profoundly changed their way of being in the world. The ancient Egyptians saw such close parallels between the archetypal adventures of the sun god during his diurnal-noctural journey, the states associated with biological death, and the experiences of neophytes in the sacred mysteries, that they considered them effectively equivalent. Modern consciousness research brings important insights into the connections and interrelations between these three experiential realms, and transfers ancient Egyptian eschatological beliefs from the world of primitive superstition to the domain of transpersonal psychology.

Liberation Through Hearing on the Afterdeath Plane: The Tibetan Book of the Dead

The Tibetan Book of the Dead, or *Bardo Thödol*, is of much more recent origin than its Egyptian counterpart, and it has incomparably more inner consistency and congruence. Unlike *Pert em hru*, it is a well-defined and homogeneous text of which we know the author and the approximate time of origin. Although it is clearly based on a much older oral material, it was first put into writing in the eighth century AD, and it is attributed to the Great Guru Padmasambhava. This legendary spiritual teacher introduced Buddhism into Tibet and laid the foundations for Vajrayana, a unique amalgam of Buddhist teachings and elements of an ancient indigenous tradition, called Bon, that had been Tibet's principal religion prior to Padmasambhava's arrival.

Little is known with certainty about the pre-Buddhist religion of Tibet; however, one of its dominant features seems to have been preoccupation with the continuation of life after death. It included elaborate rituals aimed at ensuring that the soul of the dead person was conducted safely to the Beyond. Sacrificed animals, foods, drinks, and various precious objects accompanied the deceased during the posthumous journey. Beside ensuring the happiness of the deceased in the Beyond, these rites were also expected to have beneficial influence on the wellbeing of the living.

Additional characteristic features of the early indigenous Tibetan religion were the cult of local gods, especially mountain and warrior deities, and the use of trance states for oracular activities. The original Bon had significant animistic and shamanistic components. After the arrival of Buddhism into Tibet, both these religious systems coexisted, and in spite of their separate nature, showed rich crossfertilization. In practice the two have been so closely combined as to appear fused into a single belief system. The non-Buddhist elements are particularly prominent in a terrifying rite of imagined self-annihilation, as practised by certain ascetic yogis, and in the remarkable *Bardo Thödol*.

The *Bardo Thödol* is a guide for the dying and the dead, a manual to help the departed to recognize, with the aid of a competent teacher, the various stages of the intermediate state between death and rebirth, and to attain liberation. The states of consciousness associated with the process of death and rebirth belong to a wider group of intermediate states, or 'bardos'. Among the bardos are recognized the bardo state of the existence in the womb, the bardo of the dream state, the bardo of ecstatic equilibrium during deep meditation, the bardo of the moment of death (Chikhai Bardo), the bardo of the karmic illusions following death (Chönyid Bardo), and the bardo of existence while seeking rebirth (Sidpa Bardo).

The Tibetan Book of the Dead is written as a guide for the dying. However, it has additional levels of meaning. According to the Buddhist teachings, death and rebirth do not happen only in connection with the biological demise and subsequent beginning of another lifetime, but occur in every moment of our existence. The states described in the *Bardo Thödol* can also be experienced in meditative states during systematic spiritual practice. This important text is thus simultaneously a guide for the dying, for the living, and for serious spiritual seekers. It is one of a series of instructions on six types of liberation: liberation through hearing, liberation through wearing, liberation through seeing, liberation through remembering, liberation through tasting and liberation through touching.

The instructions on the different types of liberation were formulated by Padmasambhava and written down by his wife. Padmasambhava buried these texts in the Gampo hills of central Tibet, as was done with many other texts and sacred objects, called *termas* or 'hidden treasures'. He gave the transmission of power to discover them to his twenty-five chief disciples. The texts of the *Bardo Thödol* were later found by an incarnation of one of these disciples, Karma Lingpa who belonged to the Nyingma tradition. They have been used throughout the centuries by serious students of this teaching as important guides to liberation and illumination.

The *Bardo Thödol* describes the experiences that one encounters at the time of death (Chikhai Bardo), during the period of facing the archetypal visions and karmic illusions following death (Chönyid Bardo), and in the process of seeking rebirth (Sidpa Bardo).

The Bardo of the Moment of Death

The Chikhai Bardo describes experiences associated with the moment of death, whose most characteristic feature is a sense of losing touch with the familiar world of polarities such as good and evil, and entering a realm of unreality and confusion. The logical and ordered world that we know from everyday life starts to dissolve, and there follows the sense of uncertainty whether one is attaining enlightenment or becoming insane. The *Bardo Thödol* describes the experiences heralding imminent death in terms of the different elements of the body.

Here belong experiences of heaviness, intense physical pressures, and progressive loss of touch with the physical world. In this situation, one takes refuge in the mind, and tries to reach reassurance that it is still functioning. This is described as *earth sinking into water*. In the next stage, the operations of the mind cease to be fluid and the circulation of thoughts is disturbed. The only way to relate is through emotions, to think of somebody one loves or hates. Feelings of clammy cold are replaced by sensations of fiery heat. The *Bardo Thödol* refers to this experience as *water sinking into fire*. Then the vivid emotions dissolve and attention moves away from the objects of love and hatred; one's entire being seems to be blown into atoms. This experience of *fire sinking into air* creates a state of openness for the following encounter with cosmic luminosity.

At the actual moment of death, one has an overwhelming vision of Dharmakaya, or the Primary Clear Light of Pure Reality. It is as if the whole of existence suddenly appeared in its absolute totality and in an entirely abstract form. In this experience, all dualities are transcended. Agony and ecstasy, good and evil, beauty and ugliness, burning heat and freezing cold, all coexist in one undifferentiated whole. Ultimate enlightenment and total insanity seem to be equally plausible interpretations of this experience. In the last analysis, the Dharmakaya is identical with the experiencer's own consciousness, which has no birth and no death, and is by its very nature the Immutable Light.

According to the *Bardo Thödol*, if one recognizes this truth and has been prepared by systematic practice for the immensity of this experience, the vision of the Dharmakaya offers a unique opportunity for instant spiritual liberation. Those who let themselves be deterred, and shy away from the Dharmakaya, will have another chance immediately after death when the Secondary Clear Light dawns upon them. If they miss this opportunity as well, they will be involved in a complicated sequence of spiritual adventures with an entire pantheon of blissful and wrathful deities, during which their consciousness becomes progressively more estranged from the liberating truth as they are approaching another rebirth. These are the experiences described in the texts relating to the second and third bardos.

The Bardo of Experiencing Reality

The experiences in the Chönyid Bardo consist of successive visions of a rich panoply of divine and demonic presences that one encounters during one's journey from the moment of death to the time of seeking rebirth. On the first five days of this bardo appear the glorious images of the five Peaceful Deities. These are the transcendental Dhyani Buddhas, or Tathagatas, enveloped in brilliant lights of different colours — Vairocana (Buddha

The germinal mandala of the Tibetan Book of the Dead: the mandala of the five transcendent Dhyani or Tathagata Buddhas

Supreme and Eternal), Akshobhya (Immovable Buddha), Ratnasambhava (Buddha of Precious Birth), Amitabha (Buddha of Infinite Light), and Amoghasiddhi (Buddha of Unfailing Success). With them appear their attendants, male and female Bodhisattvas.

On the sixth day, all the Dhyani Buddhas appear at once with their attendants, together with the four wrathful Door-keepers and their female partners, shaktis or dakinis, the Buddhas of the six realms or *lokas* into which one can be reborn, and a number of additional divine figures, forty-two deities altogether. Their radiances are in vivid contrast with the lure of the dull and illusory lights representing the six *lokas*. On the seventh day, five Knowledge-holding Deities from the paradisean realms appear with their dakinis, innumerable heroes and heroines, celestial warriors, and faith-protecting deities. Radiances of colourful light emanating from their hearts compete with the dull light of *tiryaloka*, the realm of animals, or brutal subhuman creatures.

The period between the eighth and fourteenth day is the time for the appearance of the Wrathful Deities. The demonic figures appearing between the eighth and twelfth day, as terrifying as they might seem, are in actuality the dark aspects of the five transcendental Dhyani Buddhas. On the thirteenth day, the Kerimas, the Eight Wrathful Ones, and the animal-headed Htamenmas emerge from within one's brain-centre. On the fourteenth day appears a rich array of deities, among them four Female Door-keepers with animal heads and other powerful goddesses, and yoginis (female yogis).

14

Block-print mandala of the Peaceful and Wrathful Deities according to the doctrine of the Tibetan Book of the Dead. The Adibuddha Samantabhadra appears at the centre, but the other deities appear only in the form of sound-syllables or mantras

For the unprepared and uninitiated, the Wrathful Deities are a source of abysmal awe and terror. However, those familiar with these images from their previous studies, and prepared for them by intensive spiritual practice, would be able to recognize them, and realize that they are essentially empty images of their own mind. They will be able to merge with them, and attain Buddhahood.

The Bardo of Seeking Rebirth

Those who have missed the opportunity for liberation in the first two bardos have to face this last stage of the intermediate state. After having fainted in fear in the Chönyid Bardo, they now awaken in a new form – the bardo body. The bardo body differs from the gross one we know in everyday life. It is not composed of matter, and has many remarkable qualities. It is endowed with the power of unimpeded motion and can penetrate through solid objects.

Those who exist in the form of the bardo body can appear and disappear at will, or travel instantaneously to any place on earth. They can change size and shape, and replicate their form, manifesting simultaneously in more than one location. At this point, one might seem to be in command of miraculous powers; here the *Bardo Thödol* issues a serious warning against allowing oneself to feel desire for these forces, and becoming attached to them.

The quality of experiences in this bardo – the degree of happiness or misery – depends on the karmic record of the dead person. Those who have

15

Painting from an initiation chart with a group of animal-headed *Phram-men-ma* deities, enveloped in auras of flame and making characteristic gestures or mudras

accumulated much bad karma will be tormented by frightening encounters with flesh-eating demons or *rakshasas* swinging weapons, terrible beasts of prey, and raging elemental forces of nature – clashing and crumbling rocks, angry overflowing seas, roaring fires, or ominous crevices and precipices. Those who have accumulated karmic merit will experience various delightful pleasures, while those with neutral karma will face colourless dullness and indifference.

A culmination of the experiences in the Sidpa Bardo is the scene of judgment, during which the Lord and Judge of the Dead, whose name is Yama Raja or Dharma Raja, examines the past actions of the individual with the help of his tale-telling mirror. He then assigns the person according to his or her merits and demerits to one of the six *lokas* or realms into which one can be reborn.

When the lights of the six *lokas* are dawning on the person at this stage of the bardo journey, an attempt can be made to close the door of the womb and prevent reincarnation. The *Bardo Thödol* suggests several approaches to this end. It might help to contemplate one's tutelary deity or meditate on the Clear Light, realize the essential voidness of all the apparitions, or focus on the chain of good karma. Another approach is to avoid attraction by figures of male and female bodies in sexual union, or resist the ambivalent oedipal forces that draw one toward one's future parents.

If all the opportunities for liberation have been missed, one will be manœuvered irresistibly by vivid illusions, and rebirth will invariably follow. With proper guidance, the unfortunate individual has one more hope left: he or she can still have some influence on the choice of the womb to enter. With the right environment and support, the new life may offer opportunities for spiritual practice that will provide a better preparation for the next journey through the bardo states.

The Ballgame in the Underworld: The Maya Book of the Dead

The ancient Maya were a high civilization with a rich cultural heritage; however, much of their literary legacy has been lost for posterity. This is partially due to the climate of Central America, an unfortunate combination of heat and moisture which is certainly not favourable for the preservation of perishable documents. However, the main responsibility for this situation falls on the Spanish invaders, who deliberately destroyed enormous quantities of literary treasures. This was particularly the case with the so-called codices, accordion-like bark-paper screenfolds with rich and colourful illustrations, a goldmine of information about various aspects of Maya life. No codices survive from the Classical Period (before AD 900) and only four from the Postclassical Period (900 to the Spanish Conquest).

The Maya lived their lives in sharp awareness of death. Short life expectancy, high infant mortality, and the combination of warfare and sacrificial rituals made death an ever-present reality. Much of the Maya ritual and art was dedicated to the process of death, from the soul's entrance into the underworld, called Xibalba, to rebirth and apotheosis. Maya mythology and funeral art described death as a journey whose challenges were known, and its important stages were depicted on coffins, walls, pottery, jades, and other objects that accompanied the deceased during the great transition.

In spite of this keen interest in death and dying, no specific eschatological texts comparable to the Egyptian or Tibetan Book of the Dead are known. However, mayologists Lin Crocker and Michael Coe were able to distinguish a well-defined group of vessels which they designated as 'codex-style ceramics' because the style of the painted scenes and glyphs that ornamented them resembled that of the Maya codices. They came to the conclusion that the same artists who created these masterpieces also painted the bark-paper books. Cardiosurgeon and archaeologist Francis Robicsek, a scholar who has studied the Maya funeral vases extensively, went one step further. He became convinced that these vases not only looked like the codices, but placed in the proper sequence, they formed a book-like narrative.

To verify this assumption he visited Maya archaeological sites as well as institutional and private collections world-wide. Together with anthropologist-hieroglypher Donald Hales, he made the first complete study of the

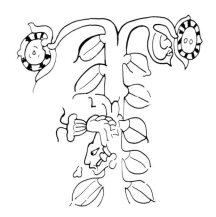

Tree bearing the head of Hun Hunahpu, the decapitated father of the Hero Twins, from a funerary ceramic

Maya codex-style ceramics, which encompassed all known examples. It became apparent that many of the vases fell into groups, each of which represented a single underworld myth or tale. Robicsek and Hales were able to suggest a tentative sequence of funerary ceramics which together represent the 'book of the dead' of the Maya.

The codex-style ceramics date from the Late Classic Period, probably around the turn of the eighth century, during the period of the greatest economic and political prosperity of the Maya city states. The scenes depicted on the vases are extremely rich and complex, painted in white, black, red and blue. They represent underworld lords and ladies with their attendants, death gods, the Hero Twins, palace ceremonies, sacrificial scenes, warfare, hunts and ritual ballgames.

Many of the vessels depict fantastic mythological creatures such as the Great Bearded Dragon, the Cauac Monster, the Hallucinatory Serpent of Bloodletting, the Principal Bird Deity, the Quadripartite Monster and the Celestial Monster. Among the animals we find jaguars, jaguar-dogs, spider monkeys, bats, rabbits, vultures, moan-birds, serpents, turtles, toads, fish, fireflies and scorpions. Some of the creatures wear sacrificial scarfs and hold bowls containing eyes, bones, and severed hands ('triadic bowls') which indicate their underworld character.

While some of these images clearly relate to myths and legends which are now lost, many of them seem to concern a famous story of the Hero Twins, who underwent incredible ordeals during their visit to Xibalba, the Maya underworld, and experienced death and rebirth. This story forms an important part of the *Popol Vuh*, an epic of the Quiché Maya put into writing shortly after the Conquest by an anonymous Guatemalan Indian, but clearly based on a much older oral tradition.

The section of the epic of particular interest in the present context describes the victorious encounter of the Hero Twins with the Lords of the Underworld, the rulers of Xibalba. The father of the Twins, Hun Hunahpu, and his companion Vucub Hunahpu were lured to the underworld by the Xibalba Lords to play ball. After their defeat they were killed and decapitated, and Hun Hunahpu's head was hung on a calabash tree. The tree, previously barren, immediately bore fruit and was hailed as miraculous.

Codex-style Maya funerary vases with creatures of the Maya underworld, Xibalba

Maya ballplayer carved on a
stone marker, with date glyphs

When a maiden named Xquic came to see the fruit, Hun Hunahpu's skull spat into her hand and impregnated her. The maiden returned to the surface of the Earth and gave birth to the Hero Twins, Hunahpu, god of the hunt, and Xbalanque, 'Little Jaguar'.

When the Twins grew up into beautiful youths, they discovered the rubber ball their father and his companion had used, and decided to descend to Xibalba to avenge their deaths. In the underworld, Hunahpu and Xbalanque were subjected to a series of perilous ordeals invented by the Xibalba Lords. They successfully overcame the dangers of the House of Gloom, the House of Knives, the House of Cold, the House of Jaguars and the House of Fire, and won against the Lords of Xibalba in all games of ball. However, in the House of Bats they almost met defeat when Hunahpu's head was cut off. The Xibalba people took the head and hung it in the ballcourt as a trophy.

Xbalanque called the animals, and the turtle took the shape of Hunahpu's head. His twin then bounced the ball far over the court, where a rabbit had been stationed to chase it and encourage the Xibalba people to run after him. Xbalanque used this diversion to steal the real head; Hunahpu was restored to life, and the game ended in a tie. During the next test, the Twins willingly jumped into the flames of a great fire, knowing that by then their prowess had won them immortality. Five days later they rose from the dead and performed miracles in the disguise of ragged fishermen. They burned houses and made them reappear, then cut themselves into pieces and returned to life looking younger and more handsome than before. When the Xibalba Lords asked the same for themselves, the Twins sacrificed them and did not bring them back to life.

The Hero Twins, Hunahpu and Xbalanque, from a painting in Naj Tunich Cave, Guatemala, Late Classic period

In the written form of the *Popol Vuh*, the Hero Twins are taken into heaven and become the sun and moon. The Maya scholar J. Eric S. Thompson believes that the written form of the epic reflects a distortion of the story under Spanish influence. He suggests that in the oral tradition, the Twins were changed into the sun and the planet Venus, considered brothers in Maya mythology. It is also likely that the original version placed a greater emphasis on the spiritual aspect of the transformation of the Twins. The legend of the Twins' father Hun Hunahpu entered the histories of various Maya sites where the rulers were regarded as the descendents or incarnations of the Hero Twins.

Although the *Popol Vuh* itself was put into writing in post-Conquest times, the legends describing the birth, life, death and rebirth of Hunahpu and Xbalanque are remnants of an important mythic cycle from the Classic Period. The Hero Twins' adventures reveal the Maya concept of the soul's journey through death and rebirth. They provided instructions for defeating death and attaining resurrection, knowledge that had universal relevance. The king, the nobles, and possibly every human being, thus metaphorically assumed at death the identity of one of the Twins.

The evidence of the codex-style ceramics thus seems to indicate that one of the Mesoamerican patterns for the posthumous journey of the soul, and possibly also for the sacred initiation of death and rebirth, was closely related to the themes of *Popol Vuh*. It portrays the transformation-process of death and rebirth as a series of difficult ordeals and adventures that take place in subterranean regions and have their characteristic protagonists. A particularly interesting and mysterious aspect of this symbolism is the element of the ritual ballgame. The ballgame was a real-life event in Mesoamerican cultures, and it seems likely it offered the living an opportunity to play out the myth of the Hero Twins.

The Mystery of the Plumed Serpent: The Nahuatl Book of the Dead

The greatest figure of Precolumbian eschatological mythology symbolizing the process of spiritual death and rebirth was undoubtedly Quetzalcoatl. This glorious deity played an important role in creation mythology. It was believed the gods created five suns in succession, each corresponding to one period of the world's history, and that Quetzalcoatl helped to create the Fifth Sun and gave it movement. He also mysteriously appeared among his people as a hero with a white complexion and a beard, who founded their religion, taught them the arts of civilization, and disappeared without trace. The myth of Quetzalcoatl was the religious theme common to all Mesoamerica.

Quetzalcoatl's name derives from two Nahuatl words: *quetzal*, a rare exotic bird of brilliant green colour, and *coatl*, a serpent. The combination of these two words literally means 'plumed serpent'. An alternative translation of the same name is Precious Twin, alluding to Quetzalcoatl's identification with the planet Venus and its two aspects as morning star and evening star. However, he was also known by many other names, such as the God of Wind, the Lord of Dawn, and Lord of the Land of the Dead. To the Mayas of Yucatan he was known as Kukulcan, closely associated with Itzamná, the deity represented as a celestial lizard or serpent with two heads.

There are two principal versions of the myth about Quetzalcoatl. The first one assumes that he was a historical figure, possibly Topilzin, a twelfth-century priest of Quetzalcoatl and the ruler of the Toltec capital of Tollan. In spite of many efforts, it has been impossible to confirm the historical authenticity of Quetzalcoatl and his adventures, and the question of his true identity has remained a deep mystery.

The second principal myth about Quetzalcoatl is an esoteric story of deep spiritual meaning, expressing a universal truth rather than historical facts. It describes Quetzalcoatl as a wise, good, and pure ruler of the City of the Gods established after the creation of the Fifth Sun. His heavenly rival and polar opposite, Tezcatlipoca, brought about Quetzalcoatl's downfall by intoxicating him with a drink of pulque, an alcoholic beverage made from the agave plant. Under its influence, Quetzalcoatl committed incest with his sister Xochiquetzal, the goddess of love and beauty. After regaining sobriety and realizing what had taken place, he imposed upon himself a harsh penance.

First he disposed of all his material riches and spent four days in a stone coffin. Then he travelled to the celestial shore of divine waters where he built a large pyre. Having donned his feathers and bird-mask, he threw himself into the flames. As he was burning, all the rare birds gathered to watch him turn to ashes. Eight days later his heart rose like a flaming star. After his physical form had died and been consumed by the fire, Quetzalcoatl underwent a journey through Mictlan, the Land of the Dead, accompanied by his twin Xolotl in the form of a dog. He succeeded in obtaining from Mictlantecuhtli, Lord of the Dead, the bones of a man and a woman, and escaped with them after many trials. He redeemed them from death with his own blood, and the first people could begin inhabiting the world.

Quetzalcoatl then made his ascent to heaven, and as Lord of Dawn was transformed into the planet Venus, the morning star. Since that time, he has been repeating his journey in this astronomical form, first appearing in the western sky as the evening star, then disappearing underground, and reappearing in the eastern sky as the morning star, to be reunited with the rising sun. The Quetzalcoatl myth is thus an expression of the universal theme of death and resurrection, sin and redemption, and the transfiguration of a human into god. Since Quetzalcoatl, as one of the four sons of the supreme Creator, was already divine when he succumbed to mortal sin, his story clearly concerns the perennial motif of all great religions: the incarnation of the pure spiritual principle as gross matter and the agonizing redemption of matter by spirit. The story of Quetzalcoatl's death, journey through the underworld and rebirth is told in the magnificent paintings of the Codex Borgia, an Aztec screenfold filled with religious and ritualistic symbolism which may be termed the Nahuatl Book of the Dead.

Quetzalcoatl's adventures in the underworld and his celestial ascent recall those in the Egyptian Book of the Dead, where the experiences of the deceased person and the initiate in the mysteries of Isis and Osiris were closely related to the noctural journey of the sun god through the underworld. But while the Egyptian version made the astronomical association exclusively to the sun, linking death with sunset and rebirth with sunrise, the Mesoamerican version included also Venus and its different phases. Venus was seen as mediator between night and day, good and evil,

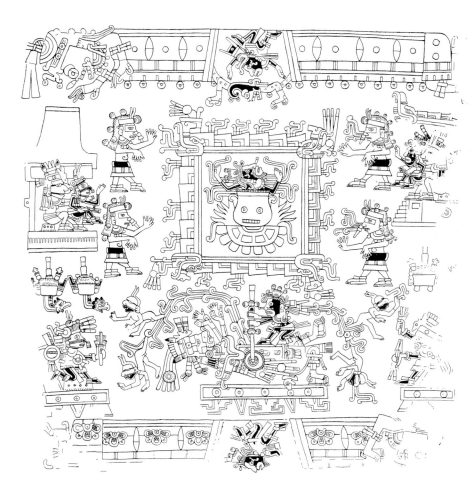

The underworld journey and transformation of Quetzalcoatl, from the 15th-century Codex Borgia. At the top, Quetzalcoatl passes through curtain formed by the body of the Earth Goddess and enters the subterranean kingdom of fire. Below, he ignites a fire in the belly of the Goddess. In the centre, he undergoes rejuvenation and solarization by fire. At the bottom, he can be seen rising in the sky in his solar aspect

and as a force facilitating transcendence of opposites within human nature.

The mythic importance of Venus for Mesoamerica is not entirely surprising for in that latitude the planet appears in the dawn sky as big as a snowball and shines with astonishing brilliance. In the Codex Borgia, as in the Mesoamerican world-view in general, mythology is intimately interwoven with astronomy. All periods of time, from hours and days to planetary orbits and phases, were seen as manifestations of cosmic forces with deep spiritual significance. In this cosmic drama, played out by a multitude of gods and goddesses, the Codex Borgia seems to reserve a special role for Quetzalcoatl, in linking his death, journey through the underworld and rebirth with the cycles of Venus.

Venus revolves around the sun in a nearly circular orbit, and during its revolution it undergoes phases, like the moon. Its sidereal period – the time of a complete orbit of the sun – is 225 days, but its synodic period, the time necessary to go through one cycle of phases, is 584 days. The Maya astronomers knew that each synodical revolution of Venus consisted of four main phases. Following the inferior conjunction with the sun, it was visible for 236 days as the morning star, until it was lost to view in the light of the sun. Then it could not be seen for ninety days until it rose again to visibility after superior conjunction, this time as the evening star. After 250 days of visibility, it passed through inferior conjunction, becoming invisible for eight days. According to myth, these eight days represented the period

Quetzalcoatl spent in the underworld before reappearing as the morning star.

The ordeals that Quetzalcoatl undergoes during his underworld journey bear a certain similarity to the descriptions of the Tibetan Book of the Dead. During his descent into Mictlan he encounters an entire pantheon of *tzitzimimes* – demons of darkness – and of wrathful deities threatening to destroy him. He also meets during his journey many peaceful deities who are nourishing, protective, and supportive. As he passes through the regions of the underworld, he is divided into two Quetzalcoatls: his dark twin brother Xolotl and his light self, Tezcatlipoca. After disintegrating into his physical, emotional, mental, and spiritual components, he transcends all the opposites, and during his transformation into Venus achieves a state of spiritual wholeness. This state has been represented in Tibet and many other cultures by the sacred symbol of the mandala. The Codex Borgia contains some of the finest mandalas of all time.

Ars Moriendi: The Christian Book of the Dead

While many people have heard about the Egyptian and the Tibetan Books of the Dead, it is generally less well known that an extensive body of literature related to problems of death and dying exists also in the western tradition. It is usually referred to as *Ars moriendi* (The Art of Dying). Toward the end of the Middle Ages the works belonging to this genre were among the most popular and widespread literary forms in many European countries, particularly Austria, Germany, France and Italy.

The intense interest in death and dying in this period of history was greatly stimulated by the general uncertainty of life in the Middle Ages. Death was ever-present, as openly visible in the cities as in the villages. People died by tens of thousands in famines, wars and epidemics. It was not exceptional that during the outbreak of pestilence a quarter, a third, or even half of an entire population would be exterminated. People were used to witnessing the deaths of their relatives, friends and neighbours. Funeral cortèges and processions with corpses were a standard part of daily life, rather than exceptional events. Mass burials, burning of cadavers, public executions, even the immolations of heretics and alleged witches and satanists were conducted on a large scale. According to some estimates, the number of the victims of the Holy Inquisition alone exceeded three million.

The all-pervading presence of death and the far-reaching corruption and disintegration of the social, political and religious fabric in medieval Europe provided the context that inspired the *Ars moriendi* literature. Both the mystical and the scholastic tradition contributed to the development of this eschatological genre, and many outstanding theologians considered its topic of sufficient significance to invest in it much time and energy. It is important to point out that the message of *Ars moriendi* was not limited to sick, old, and dying people whose main concern was biological demise. Like the Egyptian and the Tibetan Books of the Dead, the European eschatological writings addressed not only the issues related to death, but also the fundamental problems of human existence in the face of impermanence.

The extensive body of literature referred to as *Ars moriendi* falls into two broad categories. The first of these deals primarily with the significance of death in life, and would more appropriately be named *Ars vivendi* (The Art of Living). It emphasizes the importance of the right attitude toward death for life. The second focuses more specifically on the experiences of death and dying, and includes the management and emotional and spiritual support of dying people.

A recurrent theme in many of the works that belong to the category of *Ars vivendi* is *contemplatio mortis*, the contemplation of death that leads to contempt for the world and secular pursuits. This literature carries in many forms a strong reminder that a life oriented exclusively toward material goals is futile and wasted. Such an orientation is based on deep ignorance, and is possible only for those who are not aware of, or have not accepted, the fact that everything in the material world is impermanent and that death is the absolute ruler of life.

Mors certa, hora incerta (death is certain, its hour uncertain): the saying points to the awareness of death which is the beginning of all wisdom. It introduces into human life constant vigilance to avoid harmful behaviour. Our main concern should not be to live long, to prolong our life at all cost and by all possible means, but to live rightly, in accordance with divine law. Since none of us knows when death will strike us, we should live every moment of our lives as if it were the last.

This does not necessarily mean living in constant anxiety and anticipation of death. A more optimistic interpretation of such an attitude is that it reduces the degree to which we waste time and energy in the pursuit of multiple external goals, and helps us to focus instead on the fullest possible experience of the gift of life as it is manifest in the present moment. This idea is illustrated in a story by the great mythologist and philosopher Joseph Campbell. A man being pursued by a wild animal falls over the edge of a steep precipice but manages to break his fall by seizing hold of the branches of an overhanging shrub. As his grip begins to lose its strength, he notices a wild strawberry growing in a patch of grass close beside his face. He reaches out to it with his tongue, and slowly savours it. Did a strawberry ever taste as good?

The works dealing with contempt of the world illustrate the impermanence and futility of all worldly pursuits in many symbolic images, metaphors, and parables. Favourite subjects were the powerful, rich and famous, the hierarchy of Church and State. To depict those who have achieved the highest worldly goals in mortal despair at the moment of death was a devastating proof of the truth of the statement *vanitas vanitatum, omne est vanitas* (vanity of vanities, all is vanity), and, 'Thou art dust, and to dust shalt thou return'.

Memento mori – 'remember death': the strongest argument for the contempt of the flesh was the contemplation of the ugliness of death, with realistic descriptions of the human body in various stages of putrefaction and decomposition. In certain forms of meditation, medieval monks were asked to visualize their own death and identify with their bodies as they were gradually reduced to rotting flesh, bones, and finally dust. There is a reminder here of the practices of Tibetan tantric meditation in which the body is mentally annihilated, or even of more concrete exercises, where

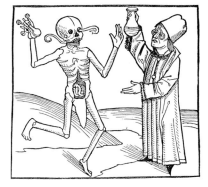

Death and the Physician, from *Der Doten Dantz mit Figuren*, 1495

The Orchestra of the Dead, from Hermann Schedel, *Liber Chronicorum*, 1493

practitioners had to meditate on corpses or in cemeteries. Modern study of non-ordinary states of consciousness has shown that exercises of this kind are much more than pathological indulgence in morbid topics. Deep acceptance of our physicality, including the worst that biological decay has to offer, leads to the realization that we are more than our body, and is a prerequisite to transcendence of the body and to spiritual opening. The message of the *Ars vivendi* was thus that we should not live purely for worldly pleasures, power and riches, which must inevitably fail us. Instead, we should learn to focus our attention on transcendental realities.

Polemic poems (*Streitgedichte*) presented the philosophical and religious problems of life and death in the form of dialogues or disputations between man and death, the world and man, life and death, the soul and the body, or the dying and the Devil. In the poems called *Vado mori* (I am walking to die), representatives of various social groups or personifications of various human characteristics shared their feelings and reflections in the face of death. These poems were in many ways predecessors of the texts used in the dances of death (*danses macabres, Totentaenze*), the fascinating medieval manifestations of mass psychology that will be discussed later in this book.

The second category of medieval works dealing with death includes texts focusing on the immediate experience of dying, and on the art of guiding and supporting dying individuals on their last journey. The beginnings of this literary genre can be traced to the end of the fourteenth century, to a time when the mortality rate from disease was so high that it became impossible for the priests to visit all the sick and prepare them for dying.

Under these circumstances, many people died, as the Church saw it, 'in the midst of their sins'. Concerned clergy became interested in disseminating information to prepare people for death before it was imminent. Among

Churchman surprised by Death. Hans Holbein, *Les simulachres et faces de la Mort*, Lyon, 1538

those who preached and taught about death were the friars of the Dominican and Franciscan orders. *Ars moriendi* at first took the form of pastoral manuals for young priests to prepare them for work with dying individuals. Later, when the number of the priests was insufficient to meet the increasing need, the Latin texts were translated into the relevant languages to make them available to lay people.

Certain parts of the texts focused on doctrinal questions for the dying and required, in accordance with tradition, specific answers. However, other parts discussed the states of consciousness experienced by the dying, and prepared them for the various challenges of the posthumous journey of the soul. Sections were also dedicated to concrete instructions for the dying and for their helpers, to guide them during the last hours. Most medieval manuals agree that the preparation for death depends critically on creating the right disposition and the right attitude in the dying person.

It was considered particularly important not to instill false hopes of recovery. All possible support should be given to the dying individual to help him or her to face death, and accept it. Confrontation with death was seen as absolutely crucial, and avoidance was considered one of the major dangers the dying person was facing. Some of the manuals explicitly stated that it was less objectionable and harmful if the helpers were to evoke fear in the dying individual, or prove to have anticipated death prematurely, rather than that they should allow him or her to use denial, and die unprepared.

The approach to the dying advocated in *Ars moriendi* was thus diametrically opposed to the practices that until recently dominated modern western medicine. In hospitals, it used to be a common practice for the attending physicians and other medical personnel to use all possible means to conceal from the patients the diagnosis and prognosis of serious diseases, and to join with the relatives in elaborate games to obscure the reality of the situation. In spite of much progress in this area, such a strategy is not exceptional even today.

The Posthumous Journey of the Soul: Myth and Science

Until the middle of this century the ancient eschatological texts and the spiritual literature in general had not received the serious attention of the western scientific circles. The interest in mysticism remained limited to individuals and groups who pursued it at the risk of isolating themselves from the mainstream culture and being ostracized. This situation started to change in the middle of this century; since that time, there has been a gradual cultural awakening in regard to spiritual matters among lay people as well as among certain groups of professionals.

Among the factors that seem to have contributed to this development were a sudden increase of interest in non-ordinary states of consciousness, triggered by scientific research and widespread popular use of psychedelics, systematic study of near-death experiences, and the discovery of powerful experiential techniques of psychotherapy. At the same time, there was also an unprecedented renaissance of interest in mysticism, Eastern philosophy and shamanism. It came as a big surprise that westerners who used psychedelics, participated in powerful forms of experiential psychotherapy, got involved in systematic meditation, or experimented with some other form of mind-altering techniques, had experiences that bore deep resemblance to those described in the mystical literature and in Eastern spiritual philosophies.

It has become obvious that the lack of appreciation of the western industrial world for the mystical traditions (or for perennial philosophy, in Aldous Huxley's sense) arose from the fact that we have lost contact with the deeper levels of our psyches that reveal themselves in altered states of consciousness. Crosscultural research has shown that the vast majority of ancient and pre-industrial cultures held non-ordinary states in great esteem, and spent much time and energy to develop various techniques of inducing them. They used them in various ritual contexts to connect with their deities and with nature, to diagnose and heal diseases, to cultivate extrasensory perception, and to tap deep sources of creative inspiration. As a result their cosmology, philosophy of life, mythology and spirituality reflected, not just everyday perception of the world, but the insights from their visionary states.

In comparison, western psychiatry pathologized all non-ordinary states of consciousness with the exception of dreams, and instead of studying them, focused on developing means of suppressing them. This resulted in a narrow, pragmatically biased understanding of the human psyche and ignorance of its true nature, as well as a limited and skewed image of the cosmos. When the experiential realm of non-ordinary states of consciousness opened to modern westerners, the typical result was a profound shift from a mechanistic world-view to a basically mystical way of understanding existence.

In addition, startling revolutionary advances in many scientific disciplines showed the limitations of the Newtonian-Cartesian mechanistic thinking and replaced it with radical alternatives. Here belong, for example, the profound revision in our understanding of the physical world brought about by the theories of relativity and quantum physics, the holographic model of the universe and of the brain as developed by David Bohm and Karl Pribram, Rupert Sheldrake's concept of morphogenetic fields in biology, Gregory Bateson's systems approach to reality, and many others. One of the most exciting characteristics of this development has been a progressive convergence between this new understanding of the universe, often referred to as the new paradigm in science, and the world-view of the mystical traditions, which has created an atmosphere conducive to serious and unbiased study of the spiritual legacy of humanity.

Modern consciousness research

Systematic study of non-ordinary states of consciousness has shown that the model of the human psyche used in traditional psychiatry and psychology, which is limited to postnatal biography and the Freudian individual unconscious, is too narrow and superficial. In deep meditation, psychedelic sessions, experiential psychotherapy, trance states, spontaneous psychospiritual crises ('spiritual emergencies'), and other similar situations, the experiences typically transcend biography, and the psyche reveals its deeper dynamics. This results in a rich spectrum of phenomena that bear a close similarity to those described in spiritual literature of all ages.

An important group of these deeper experiences combines in a very unusual way the elements of a shattering encounter with death and a struggle to be born. Since many people feel that the source of the sensations and emotions involved in these states is the memory of the birth trauma, we can refer to this level of the psyche as 'perinatal'. The activation of this domain of the unconscious – deliberate or spontaneous – results in profound experiences of dying and being born or reborn. Their rich symbolic imagery is often indistinguishable from the descriptions found in the spiritual scriptures of the world, particularly in various eschatological texts. Perinatal experiences represent a strange amalgam that combines concrete memories of biological birth with elements that are clearly archetypal and transpersonal in nature, and have a very strong spiritual overtone. They occur in four typical experiential clusters, or basic perinatal matrices, that seem to be closely related to the consecutive stages of delivery.

The first of these matrices can be referred to as the experience of the amniotic universe. Its biological basis is the situation of the original symbiotic unity with the maternal organism during foetal existence, before the onset of delivery. Besides taking the form of a biological memory, it can also be associated with oceanic or cosmic experiences and states of mystical unity. Visionary states of this kind often bring images of paradises or heavens of different cultures emerging from the collective unconscious. Reliving of episodes of intrauterine distress or crisis is often accompanied by images of treacherous demons.

The second perinatal matrix is characterized by experiences of cosmic engulfment and 'no exit' or hell. It is related to the memory of the stage of delivery when the uterine contractions encroach upon the foetus and the cervix is not yet open. The beginning of labour is experienced subjectively as a dangerous whirlpool, or as entering an ominous underworld labyrinth. When this state is fully developed it feels like a claustrophobic nightmare, a situation of extreme physical and emotional suffering from which there is no way out. Any contact with the divine seems forever lost, and all of existence appears to be meaningless, absurd, and monstrous. In spiritual terminology, this is hell or the dark night of the soul. This cluster of experiences can be accompanied by archetypal images of devils and infernal scenes from different cultures.

Many of the aspects of the third perinatal matrix can be understood from its connection with the propulsion through the birth canal after the cervix opens. It is subjectively experienced as a determined death-rebirth struggle. Among its characteristics are crushing pressures, tensions and streaming energies, pains in different parts of the body, suffocation, murderous aggression, strong sexual arousal, and encounter with various forms of biological material, such as blood, mucus, urine, even faeces. The accompanying symbolic visions combine elements of fierce titanic battles, sexual and sadomasochistic scenes, demonic motifs, scatological exper-iences, and encounter with purifying fire. Here subjects frequently identify with archetypal figures representing death and rebirth, such as Jesus, Osiris, Dionysus, Attis, Adonis, or Quetzalcoatl. This matrix is also closely related to the religious concept of purgatory.

Finally, the fourth perinatal matrix reflects the actual moment of birth and emergence into an entirely new form of existence. The propulsion through

An experience from the final stage of the death-rebirth process in a high-dose LSD session. This encounter with a Moloch-like deity with a furnace-belly and tearing claws immediately preceded psychological rebirth and the opening into light (solarization)

the birth canal is completed and is followed by explosive relief and relaxation. Subjectively, this sequence is experienced as psychospiritual death and rebirth. Emotional and physical suffering culminates in an experience of total annihilation on all the levels — physical, emotional, intellectual, moral and transcendental. This sense of ultimate disaster, usually referred to as the ego death, is typically followed by visions of blinding white or golden light, intricate rainbow halos and peacock designs, or glorious celestial beings. There is a sense of spiritual liberation, divine epiphany, redemption, and salvation. The universe seems indescribably beautiful and radiant, and evil appears ephemeral and unimportant.

Beyond the perinatal level of the psyche, as revealed in non-ordinary states of consciousness, is a domain which is now called transpersonal. This realm connects the individual psyche with the collective unconscious of all humanity, with all of nature, and with the entire cosmos. Transpersonal experiences can involve encounters with deities and demons of different cultures, spirit guides and power animals, various archetypal sceneries and mythological sequences, out-of-body states, past life memories, and many others. Phenomena of this kind have been described in different combinations in the literature on shamanism, rites of passage, Eastern spiritual philosophies, ancient death-rebirth mysteries, and specifically in the books of the dead and other eschatological texts.

Scientific exploration of the Beyond

Modern consciousness research has validated many of the claims of the great mystical traditions. It has shown that the spiritual scriptures, rather than being products of primitive minds dominated by wishful and magical thinking, describe with great accuracy experiences in non-ordinary states of consciousness. This general insight was then complemented by very specific corroboration of many of the assertions of the ancient eschatological texts. The relevant information was accumulated by thanatology, a new discipline studying death and dying.

As mentioned earlier, this field of inquiry was brought to the attention of the general public, as well as professional circles, by the 1975 publication of *Life After Life* by Raymond Moody. The author, a physician and psychologist, analyzed 150 accounts by people who had had near-death experiences, and personally interviewed some fifty people who had survived clinical death. He was able to show great similarities between the reports of his subjects and the descriptions of the posthumous journey of the soul found in the spiritual literature, from Plato through the Tibetan Book of the Dead to the writings of Emanuel Swedenborg.

Although his report was mostly anecdotal, it served as an incentive for carefully conducted systematic research of the near-death phenomena. It led to the publication of such widely read books as Kenneth Ring's *Life At Death* and *Heading Toward Omega*, Michael Sabom's *Recollections of Death*, and Bruce Greyson and Charles Flynn's *The Near Death Experience*. This information also captured the attention of the media; it has become the subject of many magazine articles and talk shows and has provided inspiration for many Hollywood movies, such as Resurrection, Flatliners, and Ghost. A study conducted in the early 1980s by Gallup Poll and reported in the book *Adventures in Immortality* by George Gallup, Jr., showed that about eight million Americans living at that time reported having had near-death experiences.

The general public is now familiar with the cartography of the near-death experience, at least on a superficial level. It is well known that about one third of the people who have a close brush with death report that it was a fantastic visionary adventure that involved such elements as a condensed life review, travel through a dark tunnel, meeting with dead relatives and ancestors, encounter with a source of light of supernatural brilliance and beauty, and a scene of divine judgment. Less frequent are memories of terrifying and hellish experiences and encounters with archetypal beings.

Probably the most interesting aspect of near-death experiences is the incidence of out-of-body travel, during which one can perceive one's own body from above and accurately observe the rescue operations. Moreover, under these circumstances it is possible to travel to other more or less remote locations and obtain reliable information about the events unfolding there. There are even reported cases where individuals who were blind because of a medically confirmed organic damage to their optical system could at the time of clinical death temporarily see the environment and then again lost their sight when they were brought back to life. Occurrences of this kind, unlike most of the other aspects of near-death phenomena, can be subjected to objective verification. They thus represent the most convincing proof that what happens in near-death experiences is more than the hallucinatory phantasmagoria of physiologically impaired brains. The similarity between these observations and the descriptions of the bardo body in the Tibetan Book of the Dead is truly astonishing.

Modern consciousness research has thus shown that the ancient sacred scriptures, including the eschatological texts, are not irrelevant products of superstition and primitive imagination. Instead, they seem to be accurate descriptions of the experiential territories traversed in non-ordinary states of consciousness. They are often based on countless personal experiences and on many centuries of careful observations. Experiential confrontation and knowledge of the realms they describe is a matter of extreme relevance, since the degree to which we become familiar and comfortable with them can have far-reaching consequences for the quality of our life, as well as for the way we die. In this sense, the books of the dead explored in this volume can be seen, not as historical curiosities, but as practical guides for situations we all might encounter sometime in the future.

Painting recording the experience of identification with the archetypal image of the phoenix, at the moment of psychological rebirth during a psychedelic session

The principal deities and archetypal beings who are encountered between the moment of death and the time of seeking rebirth are depicted together in this painting. In the centre is the Buddha Heruka, the wrathful transformation of Samantabhadra, with four other terrifying Herukas. Around them dance the fierce dakinis and guardian deities of the mandala. The small mandalas in the corners each contain one of the five transcendental Dhyani Buddhas, or Tathagatas, with their consorts and entourage of assistant Bodhisattvas. Immediately above the main circle is Vairocana, the primal Tathagata Buddha, radiating dazzling blue light from the heart. (Tibetan tanka painting, 19th century)

The contemplation of death was a central theme for the artists of the medieval *Ars moriendi* (The Art of Dying). 'And I looked and behold a pale horse, and his name that sat on him was Death.' Here Death's arrows spare the old and the poor, but strike down lords and ladies, bishops and popes in the prime of their lives. Bruegel's painting (*following page*) shows a skeleton army advancing through a panoramic scene of destruction and sudden death in many forms. As the least perishable part of the body, the skeleton and bones are cross-cultural symbols of death and the underworld deities. *Above*, a Precolumbian death god is recognizable by his fleshless limbs and skeletal backbone. (This page: Francesco Traini, fresco in the Campo Santo, Pisa, 14th century. Relief from Izapa, Mexico, c. 200 BC–AD 200. Following page: Pieter Bruegel, *The Triumph of Death*, 16th century)

The basic dilemma of human existence – how to find meaning in life, in the face of death and impermanence – is graphically illustrated by the medieval Wheel of Life. From infancy to old age and death, the wheel turns remorselessly full circle, while Death towers over the globe as absolute ruler. The Tibetan 'Wheel of Becoming' is held in the fierce grip of Yama, Lord of Death (*opposite*). At the centre, the three animals represent the forces that perpetuate the cycles of death and rebirth: pig (ignorance), rooster (desire) and serpent (aggression). In the next circle are the dark, descending, and light, ascending paths travelled by souls between lifetimes, according to their good or bad karma. The segments of the large circle represent the six realms or *lokas* into which one may be born: from the top, clockwise, the realms of the gods, titans, hungry ghosts, hell, animals and human beings. (Anonymous woodcut, 1558. Tanka painting, 18th–19th century)

In the Christian tradition of the *Ars moriendi* the gruesome and repulsive fate of the body after death has often been emphasized in order to turn people's minds from worldly and ultimately futile concerns to spiritual and transcendental realities. The painting shows the flesh whose pleasures the lovers enjoyed in their lifetimes infested with worms, toads, flies and scorpions. During the modern celebrations of the Day of the Dead, the living welcome the souls of the departed into their midst. Death symbolism abounds, but it is not meant to evoke fear or loathing; its origins lie in the autumn–winter festival of the turning year. (Master of the Sterzing Panel, *The Damned Lovers*. Players of El Teatro Campesino celebrating the Day of the Dead, San Juan Bautista, California)

Death presides over the infernal realms and their archetypal demonic beings. Yama, Tibetan Lord and Judge of the Dead, rules in a pavilion and court adorned with human skulls, heads and flayed skins. In his right hand he holds the sword symbolic of spiritual power. In the hell-scene around and below, his helpers slash, pierce or strangle those whose evil deeds were motivated by anger. Skeletal death embraces the Christian Hell, *above*, a realm of eternal torments from which no escape is possible, and where contact with the divine is forever lost. The sense of chaos, anguish, and despair of the hell experience is well conveyed by the helpless, tumbled bodies in van Eyck's painting. (Tanka painting, *c.* 1800. Detail of the Last Judgment, by Hubert van Eyck, *c.* 1426)

Visions of celestial, wrathful and demonic beings are common to all religious traditions, although the iconography the Books of the Dead shows many variations. A painting of the Last Judgment sets the Christian pantheon of God the Father, Christ and the Virgin Mary in a mandorla-shaped opening in the heavens, among saints and angels, with Satan in Hell below.

The Mandala of the Peaceful and Wrathful Deities (*opposite*) is specifically based on the *Bardo Thödol*, and is intended for mental preparation for the visionary encounters experienced at the time of dying. It centres on the 'Knowledge-holding' deity Chemchok Heruka, in the embrace of his consort. In the upper part of the mandala are the Peaceful Deities, while all around dance the ferocious host of human and animal protectors. (The Last Judgment, Bologna. Tanka painting, 18th–19th century)

Throughout history, many spiritual traditions have developed powerful techniques that make it possible to experience states of consciousness normally only accessible at the time of biological death. In some instances these approaches involved procedures damaging to the body. Some Christian mystics, for instance, spent long periods in solitude, exposing themselves to extremes of heat in the desert, or to excessive fasting and ascetic penances. Others practised various forms of painful self-mutilation. Cranach's painting shows St Jerome beating his side with a heavy stone.

The ancient Mayans employed ritual blood-letting as a powerful mind-altering method. A Maya lintel depicts Lady Xoc, wife of a ruler, experiencing a ritually induced hallucinatory vision. In her left hand she holds a dish containing blood-spotted papers and ritual lancets. Above a second dish, placed on the ground, rises a Vision Serpent, the Maya symbol for their contact with the otherworld of the gods and ancestors. From the Serpents' upper mouth emerges an armed warrior, and from another mouth below, a head of Tlaloc, deity of rain and abundance. (Lucas Cranach, *St Jerome*, 1502. Lintel, Yaxchilan, Chiapas, Mexico, Late Classic Period, AD 600–900)

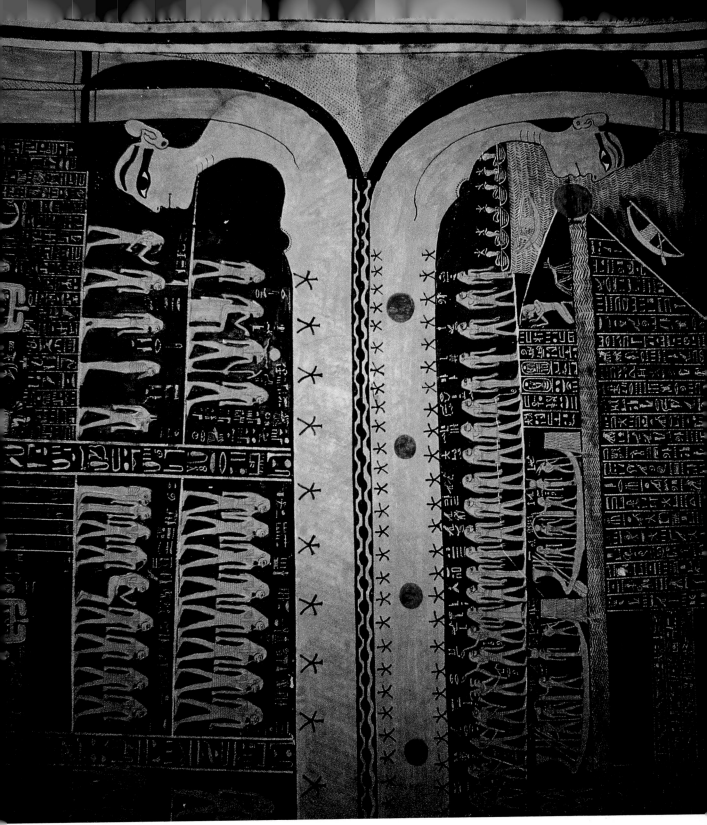

For the ancient Egyptians, the experiences of the deceased person and initiate were closely related to the nocturnal journey of the sun. Illustrating the 'Book of Day' (*left of the picture*) and 'Book of Night' (*right*), a tomb ceiling-painting represents the sun's night-time journey as a passage through the body of the sky goddess Nut. During the day, the sun disc travels west, until it reaches the goddess's mouth and is swallowed. Engulfed, it travels through the night hours to be born from her loins at daybreak into the eastern sky. (Painted ceiling, tomb of Rameses VI, 20th Dynasty)

In the Aztec Codex Borgia the final episode in the miraculous transformation of Quetzalcoatl – his death, underworld journey and rebirth as the Morning Star – is shown as occurring within the body of the goddess of death, Mictlantecuhtli, here represented by the square. In the dark abyss of the centre are shown two intertwined figures of the dead Quetzalcoatl, enclosed by the circle of his feathered neck-ornament. Below, the body of the goddess opens, giving the same two figures triumphant birth into the south-eastern sky. (Codex Borgia, p. 30)

According to Christian doctrine human beings are endowed with a single soul which parts from the body at the time of death and has to face the consequences of the individual's actions. Depending on how well prepared the individual is for the ordeals of death, and upon the outcome of a divine judgment, it will be directed to heaven, hell or purgatory. The medieval scene of a death chamber indicates the trials that may be expected during the last hours. It shows an angel and the devil hovering above the dying man's head, waiting to contend for his departing soul. (Illumination from the Grimani Breviary, 1480–1520)

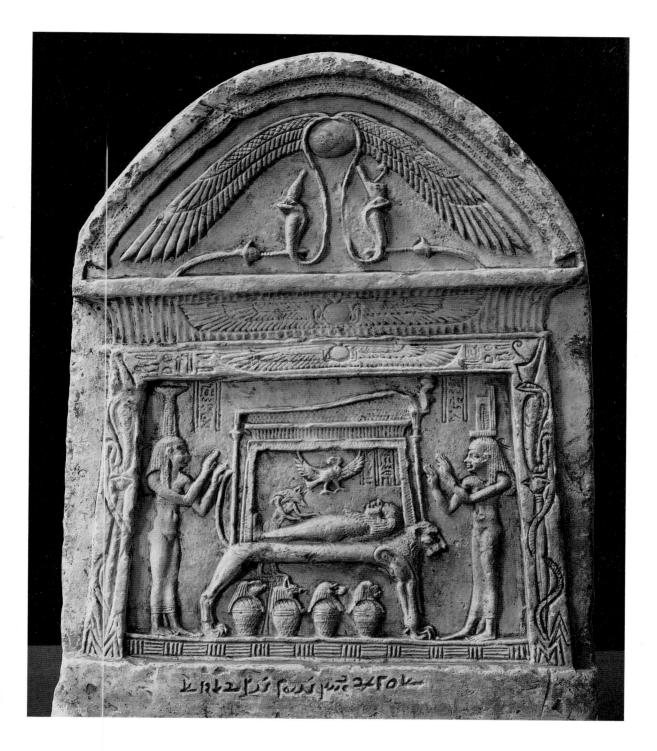

The ancient Egyptian conceptions of the soul were considerably more complex. The spiritual aspect of each person was believed to consist of several main components. Of these, the *ka* was the vital force that leaves the body at the time of death and travels west to meet its heavenly double in the kingdom of Osiris, afterwards dwelling both in paradise and in the tomb. *Ab* was the conscience or 'heart', which faced the judgment. *Akh* was the transfigured spirit. *Ba* was the power of animation after death: here Osiris's *ba* is shown hovering over his mummy at his embalmment. (Relief, 23rd Dynasty)

Water plays an important role in death-rebirth mythology. For the ancient Maya, the moment of death was sometimes equated with the downward plunge of a canoe. The serrated outline of an eccentric flint suggests both the dive of a canoe with its passengers into the watery underworld, and the shape of an underworld water-creature, the crocodilian Celestial Monster.

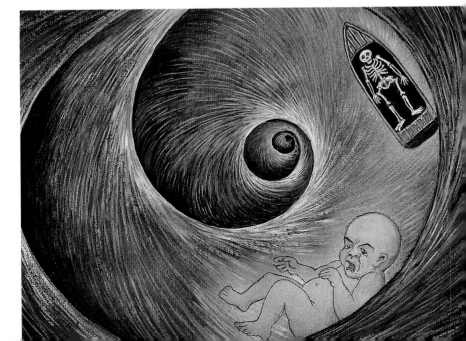

The element of water also dominates a painting from a psychedelic session which captures the subject's experience of the onset of psychological death and rebirth. It shows a whirlpool drawing the helpless foetus into its centre and threatening to engulf and annihilate him.

The Egyptian Book of the Dead describes the sun god's journey through the dark regions of the underworld as a voyage on subterranean waters, involving many perils and ordeals. In this section, Ra takes the form of a ram-headed human figure. A serpent known as 'the Enveloper' forms the deck-cabin over him. An esoteric meaning of the underworld journey is the transformation from the densest form of matter to the most subtle form of energy, followed by re-emergence into the material world. (Eccentric flint from North Petén, Guatemala, 650–800. Contemporary psychedelic painting. Wall painting from the tomb of Sethos, Abydos, c. 1285 BC)

54

The divine judgment of the soul appears in the ancient Egyptian, Tibetan and Christian accounts of the afterlife as a scene of weighing. In Christian doctrine the soul is judged at the time of death and again on the Day of Doom. A cathedral sculpture (*left*) shows the Archangel Michael and the Devil weighing the souls, and competing for them at the Last Judgment. The Devil is evidently cheating.

According to the Egyptian Book of the Dead, the judgment took place in the underworld Hall of Maat, goddess of justice. First came a 'negative confession', in which the deceased declared that he or she had committed no sins. Then the deceased (shown standing at the left) watches as her *ab* or 'heart', seat of conscience, is weighed against a feather, or here, against a small figure of Maat.

Horus attends the balance, and Thoth, the scribe of the dead, acts as an impartial witness. Below the scale waits Amenet, Devourer of Souls, a crocodile-headed monster who swallows any heart heavy with sin. Those whose hearts pass the judgment are led by Horus to join Osiris in the paradise of the Happy Fields. (Sculpture by Gislebertus, Autun Cathedral, c. 1132. Judgment from a papyrus Book of the Dead)

The archetypal beings of heaven and the underworld are often seen as endowed with wings. Isis, the Great Mother Goddess, enchantress, and sister and spouse of Osiris, who took the form of a kite to conceive his son Horus, stands as protectress in the shrine of the pharaoh Tutankhamen, with long golden wings outspread. (Relief, tomb of Tutankhamen, 18th Dynasty)

The joyous scene of the Coronation of the Virgin as Queen of Heaven (*opposite*) is thronged with gold-winged beings. Gold is frequently used as a metaphor for the visionary and paradisean state, while wings denote unlimited ability to travel between realms, or else divine kindness and protectiveness. (The Limbourg brothers, *Les Très Riches Heures du duc de Berri*, 1409–15)

The hope of resurrection or re-incarnation – of new life after the darkness of death, finds expression in a variety of different metaphors. A painting from a psychedelic session in which a tree's roots are shown drawing nourishment from a coffin, recalls the myth of the dead Osiris concealed in the trunk of a beautiful tree until he was discovered by his sister-spouse Isis. A relief (*below*) from the Temple of Dendera shows Osiris's coffin enclosed in a tamarisk tree. Both images reflect the insight that life feeds on life, and new life grows out of old. For medieval faith (*right*), the dead rose in their bodies on Judgment Day, in a literal awakening of the dead, to clamber gratefully out of their dark tombs. (Contemporary psychedelic painting. Drawing after a relief at the Temple of Dendera, 1st century BC. Illumination from the Vyšehrad Gospel Book, 11th century)

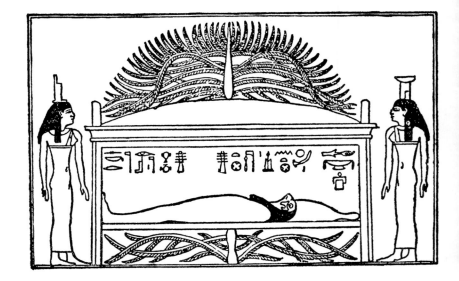

The realms of Paradise, the abodes of the blessed, typically combine the most beautiful and pristine aspects of nature: sparkling streams and lakes, luscious vegetation, rich profusion of fruits and flowers, birds and young animals.

The paradise of the ancient Egyptians bore a striking similarity to their earthly life. The deceased Sed-nedjem and his wife are shown in the Happy Fields after their resurrection, enjoying boat-trips on the Celestial Nile and carrying on a variety of agricultural activities rewarded with magnificent harvests.

The emphasis on farming carries a profound symbolic meaning: just as plants are sown, grown, harvested, and re-emerge after a second sowing, so the deceased is reborn in the hereafter. The scene on the tympanum links the Happy Fields with the voyage of the solar barque and the emergence of the sun at dawn, and so with rebirth.

The Christian Paradise is frequently represented as a rose garden (*opposite*), an exquisite haven of peace and love for the soul after death. With the Virgin and Child is shown the martyred St Catherine of Alexandria, mystic bride of the infant Christ. The peacocks represent immortality. (Tomb of Sed-nedjem, 19th Dynasty. Madonna of the Rose Garden, by Stefano da Verona, c. 1374–1450)

Flowers form an essential element of the paradisean landscapes, and the symbolism of particular flowers is often used to describe high mystical states – in particular the rose in western tradition, and the lotus in India, the Far East and pre-Hispanic America.

A visionary drawing by William Blake illustrates the Virgin as Queen of Heaven in Glory, in the mystic white rose. Angels and sages are enfolded among the petals. A Maya ceramic represents a young lord as reborn in a waterlily, while the transcendental

Tathagata Buddha Akshobhya is represented in a bronze sculpture enthroned in a lotus, surrounded by eight Bodhisattvas couched in the petals. The lotus-flower, arising from the underwater darkness and mud of the lake bottom to open in pristine beauty in the sun, is a

particularly apt symbol for the spiritual journey. (William Blake, illustration for the *Paradiso*, Dante's *Divine Comedy*, 1824–7. Vessel of the Maya ceramic codex. Bronze mandala, East India, 12th century)

A triumphant scene from the
papyrus of Ani depicts the instant
of the emergence of the sun god
after his nocturnal journey through
the underworld. At the same time,
it represents the rebirth of the
deceased person, and the moment
of illumination of the initiate in the
mysteries. Beside the *djed*, the
vertebral column of Osiris, kneel
his sisters Isis and Nephthys,
worshipping the solar disc
supported by the *ankh*, symbol of
eternal life. The six baboons in
postures of adoration are the Spirits
of Dawn, celebrating the sunrise.
(Papyrus of Ani, 19th Dynasty,
c. 1250 BC)

Right: A fleshless sun, on its way to
light the world of the dead. (From
the Aztec Pyramid of the Sun,
Teotihuacan, Mexico, AD 500)

Themes

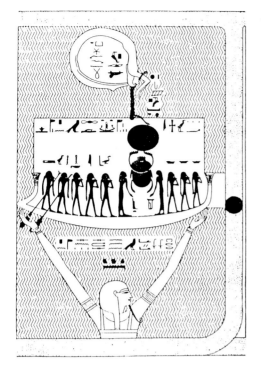

Egyptian Deities of the 'First Time'

The deities of the Egyptian Book of the Dead or *Pert em hru* are linked with the earliest times, when the cosmos itself was created. In Egyptian mythology the source of creation was Nun, god of the waters of primordial chaos. The creator of gods, humanity and the universal order was the self-created Atum; at the time of the Pyramid Texts (2350–2175 BC) Atum became identified with the sun god, Ra.

Nun appears, *left*, at the moment of creation, upholding the solar barque with the sun god in the form of a scarab who supports the rising sun. On either side of the sun god stand the goddesses Isis and Nephthys, and the boat carries additional deities who assist the sun god during his dangerous journey. Above is shown the sky goddess, Nut, receiving the new sun; she stands on the head of Osiris, whose body encircles and embraces the 'lower world' or Duat.

The first divine couple, Shu, god of air and empty space, and Tefnut, goddess of life-giving moisture, conceived the earth god Geb and the sky goddess Nut. The siblings showed each other great affection, defying the strict prohibition of their father. *Below*, Shu is seen upholding his daughter Nut (the vault of the sky) in the attempt to keep her forever separate from his son Geb (earth).

While the jealous Ra also tried to keep them separate, Nut and Geb were brought together by the god Thoth. Playing draughts with the moon, he won a 72th portion of his light, and on these five days stolen from the lunar

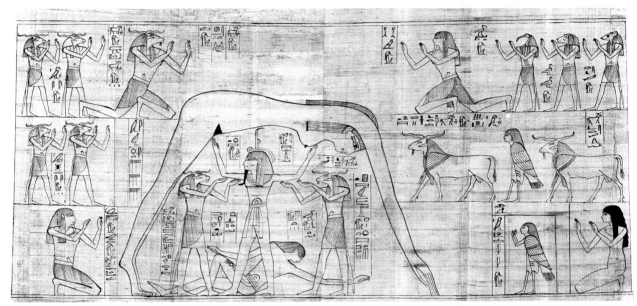

calendar, Nut and Geb were able to conceive their four children, the divine siblings Osiris, Isis, Seth and Nephthys. A funerary papyrus, *bottom left*, shows the sisters Isis and Nephthys praising the sun god Ra as he rises in the east. Between them is the *djed* pillar which symbolized the spinal column of Osiris, the seat of the magic fluid and the vital fire of life, bestowed by Osiris on the dead. Below the vault of heaven stands the sun god Ra in the form of a falcon.

Osiris, an ancient corn deity, was associated from earliest times with funerary rites and the pattern of birth, death and renewal. Eventually he came to represent for his followers the hope of an eternally happy life in another world, where he ruled as a good and just king. He is depicted here (*facing, bottom right*) with his sister and spouse, Isis. Her name means 'seat', and she is often shown wearing a little throne on her head. Osiris was traditionally represented as a dead king, with only the hands emerging from the mummy's wrappings, holding the emblems of his supreme power, a shepherd's crook and a flail.

Seth, the fourth of the divine siblings, *below left*, was an ancient deity originally worshipped in Libya in the form of a crocodile or hippopotamus. He is cast as the treacherous archenemy of his brother Osiris, but the legend gives him cause for hatred. Although he was the husband of his sister, Nephthys, her loyalties were to Osiris. Seth being the god of aridity and storms, the marriage remained childless. With the help of alcohol and disguised as Isis, Nephthys managed to conceive by Osiris her son, Anubis, who became the herald of death and inventor of embalming. Seth was usually represented as a pig-like animal with a long curving snout, square upstanding ears, and an upright tufted tail.

Another important figure from the *Pert em hru* was Thoth, a self-begotten deity who mysteriously emerged in a lotus, the inventor of speech, the sacred hieroglyphic alphabet, and also of mathematics, engineering, magic and divination. He was seen as the god of the moon and as Measurer of Time. One of his important roles was impartial judge of the dead. His symbolic representations show him either ibis-headed or as a dog-headed baboon. *Below*, he is shown bestowing eternal life on pharoah Seti I by pointing the Nile cross or *ankh* toward his nostrils. (Facing page: Drawing, relief on the sarcophagus of Seti I, 19th Dynasty, c. 1305 BC. Greenfield Papyrus, c. 950 BC. Papyrus of Hunefer, 19th Dynasty, c. 1310 BC. Papyrus of Ani, 19th Dynasty, c. 1250 BC. This page: Bronze figure of Seth, 22nd Dynasty, c. 945–715 BC. Wall painting, tomb of Seti I, 19th Dynasty, 1305–1290 BC)

The Sun's Underworld Voyage

The posthumous journey of the soul was closely associated with the diurnal-nocturnal journey of the sun god Ra, who emerged in the east from behind Manu, the mountain of sunrise, and began his journey in the Manjet boat, the Barque of Millions of Years. During the day he traversed the sky, giving heat, light, and life to the earth. At sunset, the sunboat passed through the chain of mountains in the west, and during the night, as a second barque, the Mesektet boat, continued the journey through the Tuat, the Egyptian underworld (*centre left*).

The Tuat was a gloomy and treacherous place that presented grave dangers for the solar crew. It was divided into twelve provinces, usually called *arrit* (hall), *nut* (city) and *sekhet* (field), each the equivalent of one night hour. All the halls had gates with specific watchers, heralds and gatekeepers, *top left*, who had to be correctly named with the help of the Book of the Dead before the barque was allowed to continue.

Ra and his companions had to struggle through places of blazing fire, where heat and fumes destroyed nostrils and mouths. Many hideous beings and fantastic creatures threatened them on their way. Among the perils was Osiris's brother Seth in the form of Aapep, a gigantic snake that attempted to devour the solar disc just before sunrise (p. 89).

As Ra passed along the infernal river the various gods and demons who inhabited each province came forward to haul his boat, for no wind could penetrate the Tuat. At the close of the Twelfth Hour, *left*, the sun god emerged triumphant. Here, in a scene illustrating the *Am Tuat* (The Book of What is in the Tuat) he is shown as a scarab entering the eastern sky.

The followers of the sun god assumed that the deceased and initiates joined him on the solar barque and participated in the crew's heroic adventures. For the followers of Osiris, the solar barque would carry them to the hall where Thoth held the scales of judgment, *right*, and then, provided the judgment was safely passed, they

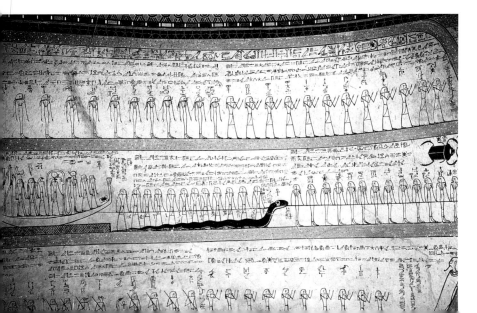

were led to Osiris's kingdom (p. 92).

The tomb of Tutmosis III, *above*, is shown painted with scenes of the First Hour of the *Am Tuat* (The Book of What is in Tuat), a guide for the deceased on the underworld voyage.

After mummification, the bodies of royal persons and nobles were often placed in a number of richly decorated anthropomorphic coffins. The cartonnage for a priest's mummy, *right*, displays the *djed* column symbol of Osiris and other imagery related to the Book of the Dead. At the tomb, the mummy was first held upright, and, before it was lowered into the sepulchre chamber, the ceremony of the 'Opening of the Mouth' was performed to allow speech at the gates and the judgement, and to ensure the rebirth of the deceased (see p. 86). (Facing page: Papyrus of Ani, 19th Dynasty, c. 1250 BC. Relief wall painting, tomb of Seti I, 19th Dynasty, 1305–1290 BC. Wall painting, tomb of Tutmosis III, Valley of the Kings, 18th Dynasty, c. 1450 BC. This page: Tomb of Tutmosis III with wall paintings, 18th Dynasty, c. 1450 BC. Cartonnage of Nespanetjerenpere, 22nd Dynasty, c. 945–715 BC. Papyrus of Kenna, 19th Dynasty, c. 1305–1290 BC)

While many religions and cultures have elaborate mythologies with vivid descriptions of deities and demons, none matches the rich and detailed iconography of Tibetan Buddhism. This is particularly reflected in the Tibetan Book of the Dead, or *Bardo Thödol*, which describes a fantastic array of blissful and wrathful deities and other archetypal inhabitants encountered on the afterdeath plane.

Authorship of this work is attributed to the legendary spiritual teacher Padmasambhava, who is credited with bringing Buddhism to Tibet. He is depicted, *above*, among various scenes from his life. The profound wisdom that can lead to spiritual liberation is known as Prajnaparamita, and is sometimes personified as a goddess (*above right*).

According to the Tibetan Book of the Dead, the best opportunity for ultimate liberation occurs at the moment of death, during the first bardo, or intermediate state between life and death. The Primary and Secondary Clear Light that manifest at this time represent the cosmic creative energy in its pure nature, and the encounter with them can be overwhelming. Should the opportunity for liberation in this bardo

be missed, progression through the remaining two bardos reveals an ever-increasing multitude of specific forms.

The five primordial expressions of cosmic energy, the Dhyani or Tathagata Buddhas, first appear in their blissful aspects (*facing page*) and gradually develop into an amazing pantheon of Knowledge-holding, Wrathful and Door-keeping Deities, Yoginis of the Four Cardinal Points, and a rich array of other archetypal beings. Simultaneously there shine the dull lights of different colours representing the six *lokas*, or realms into which one can be reborn. Lastly, the Sidpa Bardo, the Bardo of Seeking Rebirth, brings the Judgment and scenery of the *lokas*.

'Tathagata', like the name Buddha, signifies 'the Awakened One'. The five Tathagatas are the five principal modes of energy of Buddha-nature, fully awakened consciousness. They embody five qualities of wisdom; everything that is part of existence and every event can be described in terms of one of the five. However, in the state of mind of an unenlightened person, they appear as five poisons or confused emotions, represented by their wrathful aspects.

Tathagata Vairochana, 'Spreading

Forth of the Seed' (*facing page, left*), is the Buddha of the Central Realm and the first to manifest. He is white, and the space in which he appears is blue; the dazzling blue light that radiates from his heart competes for the attention with the dull white light of the Realm of Gods (*devaloka*). Seated on a lion throne and embraced by the Mother of the Space of Heaven, he holds an eight-spoked wheel symbolizing transcendence of direction and time. He represents the wisdom of the Dharmadhatu, the limitless, all-pervading space in which everything exists as it really is. Since he is the original and central figure, his family of associated Bodhisattvas is known as the Buddha or Tathagata family. In his negative aspect, he symbolizes the poison of confusion or ignorance out of which all the others evolve.

Akshobhya, 'Immovable Buddha', next to appear, is the Buddha of the Eastern Realm of Pre-eminent Happiness. He is blue, and the bright white light of the mirror-like wisdom radiating from his heart competes with the smoke-coloured light of the Hell Realm (*narakaloka*). Embraced by his consort Buddha-Locana, 'the Buddha Eye', he

sits on an elephant throne, holding a five-pronged Vajra or thunderbolt. Like all the Tathagatas, he has two male and two female Bodhisattvas as his attendants. Akshobhya is the ruler of the Vajra family that represents deep transcendental wisdom, reflecting everything with clarity and without critical judgment. The corresponding poison is aggression or hatred.

Ratnasambhava, 'Buddha of Precious Birth', is the Buddha of the Southern Realm Endowed with Glory. He is yellow and radiates the dazzling yellow light of equanimity and non-discrimination, the richness and majesty of which might make one choose the competing dull bluish-yellow light of the Human Realm (*manakaloka*). He is represented here (*top right*) as a Bodhisattva. His right hand makes the boon-bestowing gesture and his left the contemplation gesture. (Facing page: Tanka painting, 16th–17th century, Wall painting, Tholing Monastery, 15th century. This page, above: Tathagata Vairocana and consort, detail of tanka painting. Right: Ratnasambhava, bronze, 14th–15th century. Amitabha, tanka painting, 15th century, Amoghasiddhi, tanka painting, c. 18th century)

Seated on a horse-throne, Ratnasambhava is described as holding in his hand the wish-fulfilling gem. His yellow colour symbolizes the fertility, wealth, and richness of the earth; his consort Mamaki represents water, an element which is indispensable for fertility. Ratnasambhava presides over the Ratna family which is characterized by the wisdom of equanimity, equality, and non-discriminating light; its specific poison is pride.

The fourth of the blissful deities, Amitabha, 'Buddha of Infinite Light', is the Buddha of the Western Paradise or Sukhavati. He is red, and radiates from his heart brilliant red light of the all-discriminating wisdom. Simultaneously shines the dull red light of the Realm of the Hungry Ghosts (*pretaloka*). Amitabha is described as seated on a peacock throne, holding a lotus, and embraced by his consort Pandaravasini, 'the White One'. He is shown here (*previous page, centre right*) in monk's robes, with monks, Bodhisattvas, lotus pools, lions and peacocks. The peacock and the lotus symbolize purity, openness and acceptance. Amitabha rules

the Padma family, characterized by compassion and discriminating wisdom. Its poison is indulgence in ordinary passions and attachment to pleasurable aspects of the material world.

Amoghasiddhi, 'Buddha of Unfailing Success', is the Buddha of the Northern Realm of Successful Performance of Best Actions. He is green, and emanates from his heart radiant green light which competes with the dull green light from the Realm of the Jealous Gods (*asuraloka*). He is described as enthroned on a *sheng-shang*, an archetypal bird, and embraced by his consort, Samaya-Tara, 'Saviour of Sacred Word'. He holds a crossed multicoloured vajra symbolizing total fulfilment. Among his Bodhisattvas is Vajrapani, or 'Vajra-holder', symbolizing enormous energy (*below right*), shown here with his consort. Amoghasiddhi presides over the Karma family, associated with wise action, efficiency and fulfilment; the corresponding poison is jealousy. This Tathagata is shown here among numerous small representations of himself (*previous page, foot*). The repetition serves the purpose of increasing the spiritual

power of the image, as the effect of prayers is augmented by prayer-wheels or by reiteration of spoken mantras.

After the five Peaceful Tathagatas have appeared singly on the first five consecutive days of the Chönyid Bardo, they all manifest simultaneously on the sixth day (*below left*). They fill all the space, all the directions, and there is no escape, for the four gates are guarded by the Door-keepers with their consorts: the east by Vijaya, the 'Victorious One', the south by Yamantaka, 'Destroyer of the Lord of Death' (p. 74, *above*), the west by Hayagriva, the 'Horse-headed King', and the north by Amritakundali, the 'Coil of Immortality'. With them appear the Buddhas of the six *lokas* and other figures: forty-two deities altogether, depicted *opposite left* in the Mandala of the Peaceful Deities.

On the seventh day appear the Vidyadharas, or 'Knowledge-holding Deities', shown *opposite right* with the Wrathful Deities. All the deities of the *Bardo Thödol* have a specific connection with the chakras, or centres of subtle energy of the body. While the Peaceful Deities are associated with the

heart centre and the Wrathful Deities with the brow centre, the Knowledge-holders represent the link between them, mediated by speech, and are thus connected with the throat chakra. This is also reflected in their countenance and demeanour. They are not quite peaceful and not quite wrathful, but intermediary; they are majestic, impressive, and overwhelming. At the time of their appearance manifests also the green light of the Animal Realm (*tiryakaloka*), symbolizing ignorance.

The Vidyadharas are shown dancing, while making mudras (gestures) of fascination and holding crescent knives and skulls filled with blood, signifying renunciation of human life and of the world of illusion. They are surrounded by innumerable dakinis, heroes, heroines, celestial warriors, and faith-protecting deities. Using drums and thigh-bone trumpets, they produce awesome music that causes entire world-systems to tremble. Awe-inspiring mantras alternate with terrifying screams: 'Slay! Slay!'

In the centre of their circle is the Lotus Lord of Dance, the 'Supreme

Knowledge-holder Who Ripens the Karmic Fruit', in a halo of radiant rainbow colours, embraced by his dakini. In the east is the Earth-abiding Knowledge-holder', white, and embraced by the White Dakini. To the south is the smiling and radiant deity named 'He Who Has Power Over Duration of Life', yellow and with the Yellow Dakini. In the west is the 'Knowledge-holder of the Great Symbol', red, smiling and radiant, in the embrace of the Red Dakini. To the north is the 'Self-evolved Knowledge-holder', green in colour, half-angry and half-smiling, embraced by the Green Dakini.

From the eighth to the twelfth day of the Chönyid Bardo the Tathagatas appear in their horrifying aspects, as Herukas and their consorts (p. 33). They have three heads, six arms and four feet, and represent the colossal energy of the Buddha families. The dark brown Great Glorious Heruka is the terrifying aspect of Vairochana. Vajra-Heruka, dark blue, is the wrathful form of Vajrasattva (Akshobhya). The horrific aspect of Ratnasambhava is yellow Ratna-Heruka, while Amitabha Buddha's dark

counterpart is the reddish black Padma-Heruka, and that of Amoghasiddhi is the dark green Karma-Heruka. As a protection against terrifying bardo visions, the Bardo Thödol suggests visualization of Vajrapani (*facing, right*).

On the thirteenth day appear the Kerimas, the Eight Wrathful Ones, and the Htamenmas, terrifying zoomorphic deities with the heads of various animals – lion, tiger, fox, wolf, vulture, crow and owl. On the fourteenth day, the visions of this bardo end with a rich array of deities, among them four female Door-keepers with animals heads and other powerful zoomorphic deities and yoginis.

If all the opportunities for liberation in the first two bardos were missed, the process moves to the Bardo of Seeking Rebirth, with its specific challenges. (*Facing page*: detail of a mandala with the five Tathagata Buddhas and Door-keepers. Vajrapani, brass, early 15th century. This page: Mandala of the Forty-two Peaceful Deities, tanka painting, 18th century. The Great Mandala of the Knowledge-holding and Wrathful Deities, tanka painting)

The Six Realms of Existence

A central theme in the Sidpa Bardo is the judgment. The King and the Judge of the Dead (*facing page, below*) is Yama Raja, King of Death. His head and body, his pavilion and court are adorned with human skulls, heads and hides. He treads underfoot a figure symbolic of the illusory nature of human existence, and judges the dead holding in his right hand a sword, a symbol of spiritual power, and in his left the Mirror of Karma, in which are reflected all the good and evil deeds of the judged.

On either side of the balance, attended by Shinje, a monkey-headed deity, stand the Little White God (left) with a sack of white pebbles and the Little Black God (right) with a sack of black pebbles. On the instructions of Yama Raja they place on the scale white or black pebbles according to karmic merits or demerits of the judged. Various animal-headed deities act as witnesses. Issuing from the court are six karmic pathways leading to the six buddhas of the *lokas*, and below are the hells. According to the result of the weighing, the dead are assigned to one of the six realms of existence. In Tibetan Buddhist psychology, movement between the *lokas* is not limited to the time of biological death, but applies equally to deep transformation occurring in the course of spiritual practice.

The six realms are depicted as segments in the Wheel of Life (*facing page, above*). The Realm of Hell (*narakaloka*), at lower right, is a domain where one is exposed to extreme tortures, each of which represents the forces operating in one's own psyche. There are the Eight Hot Hells where mountains are made of red-hot metal, rivers are molten iron and claustrophobic space is permeated with fire. The Eight Cold Hells are regions where everything is frozen. In the hot hells are those whose acts were motivated by violent anger, while the acts resulting from selfish

motives and pride lead one to the cold hells. Other tortures involve being hacked or sawn to pieces, strangled, pierced and exposed to crushing pressures. In the horrible Avitchi Hell, those who deliberately neglected to fulfil Tantric vows endure unending tortures.

The Realm of the Hungry Ghosts (*pretaloka*) is inhabited by pitiful creatures who possess insatiable appetites. They have large distended bellies, but their mouths are the size of pinholes. In this realm, even as we gather the fruits of our desire, they make us feel more hungry and deprived. As with addiction, a fleeting experience of pleasure leads only to further endless searching. This is the suffering associated with greed.

The Animal Realm (*tiryakaloka*) is characterized by dullness, or survival on an uncomplicated level, where a sense of security alternates with fear. Whatever is unpredictable is perceived as threatening and becomes a source of confusion and paranoia. Humour is not among the features of the Animal Realm. The animals can experience pleasure and pain, but the sense of humour and irony is missing.

The Human Realm (*manakaloka*) is a domain where pleasure and pain are balanced. As in that of the Hungry Ghosts, there is the incessant passion to explore and seek pleasure. However, this *loka* also shares with the Animal Realm the tendency to operate in such a way that one creates a safe and predictable situation. A characteristic of the Human Realm is a sense of territoriality inspiring the invention of clever and cunning tools for self-protection and defeat of others. It leads to a world of tremendous success and achievement; however, when this process lacks conscious awareness, it results in a dangerous situation where people lose control of their lives.

The Realm of the Jealous Gods (*asuraloka*) is a domain entirely governed by jealousy and envy. The purpose of life in this realm is to function, survive and win in the atmosphere of intrigues. On the archetypal level, it is the world of the titans, angry warrior demigods who are in constant battle with the gods. In everyday life, it manifests as the world of international diplomacy, military leaders and politicians. One is born here as a result of intense jealousy.

The Realm of the Gods (*devaloka*) is described as a state of existence filled with delight and endless pleasures. Mythology describes heavenly and paradisean realms with gorgeous gardens, splendid palaces and abundance of brilliant gems and precious metals. This realm can be experienced in life by a consciousness suffused with loving kindness and compassion. When awareness is lacking, this domain is expressed as pride in the ego and one's separate identity, and the transient pleasures of worldly rank and wealth.

In Tibetan spiritual practice, the awareness is cultivated so that each of these experiential realms may be entered without entrapment. The essential strategy in approaching all domains of existence, whether they involve the challenges of everyday life, encounters with radiant and wrathful deities, or adventures in the various *lokas*, consists in the realization that all are ultimately products of our own mind, and that all forms are actually empty. This results in the ability to see the true reality of the Dharmakaya beyond the illusory appearances in all the domains, and on all the levels of existence. To practise this awareness during our lifetime makes it possible to use the situation of biological dying as an opportunity for instant spiritual liberation. (Facing page: Yamantaka, Doorkeeper of the South, tanka painting, 18th century. Manuscript of the *Bardo Thödol*. This page: Wheel of Becoming, painting in Tiksey Monastery, Ladakh. Judgment scene, Sikkim, 1919)

75

Death, Rebirth and the Maya Underworld

The Maya underworld, Xibalba, had landscapes and architecture, like the temples and palaces of the Lords, but the scenes painted on the funerary vases of the ceramic codex (p. 17) also indicate that it was associated with water in some important way. As with Greek mythology, the passage through the Maya underworld involved a water-crossing. Incised bones found at Tikal in Guatemala suggest the Maya there equated death with a canoe voyage. A bone, *above*, represents a canoe guided by the Paddler Twins: the Old Jaguar God in front and the Aged Stingray-spine God behind, with four animal passengers: a dog, a parrot, a spider monkey and an iguana. The human figure seated in the centre of the canoe is holding his wrist in a gesture signall-ing impending death; the glyphic symbols on his headdress identify him as the deceased Ruler A in whose mausoleum these bones were found. A

second bone, *top right*, shows a canoe at the moment of sinking below the water. Important iconographic ele-ments of the ceramic codex include sea-shells, waterlilies and alligator-like creatures.

The inhabitants of Xibalba are many and varied; they include anthropo-morphic, zoomorphic and skeletal crea-tures, as well as an entire menagerie of chthonic animals. A codex-style vase, *above*, shows God GI of the Palenque triad with four lesser gods ambushing a young lord as he emerges from the jaws of a Bearded Dragon. Fish indicate a watery *milieu*.

The god known to Mayologists as God L was clearly the principal ruler of Xibalba. He wore a Moan Bird (screech-owl) headdress, and was usually repre-sented seated on a throne. He is shown on a vase from Guatemala, *above right*, enjoying the good life with five god-desses, the Chihuateteo, the souls of

women who have died in childbirth. The goddess sitting at the left of the throne-platform turns her head to watch the scene of the beheading of a bound captive by two executioners. A snake-like form with ennucleated eyes that emerges near the victim's loins may represent a Vision Serpent. The accompanying glyphic text identifies the two executioners as the Hero Twins, Hunahpu (left) and Xbalanque (right), who entered the underworld and faced the Lords of Xibalba to avenge the deaths of their father and uncle. In the foreground a rabbit scribe is shown writing a codex.

Though in general the triumphant ending of the underworld journey in rebirth and resurrection are repre-sented in the ceramic codex far less frequently than scenes describing the ordeals of hell, splendid examples of rebirth imagery do occur. On a tripod-plate, *right*, a young lord wearing body-

jewelry and a headdress of quetzal feathers emerges from a crack in a turtle carapace. He is identified as Hun Hunahpu, the murdered father of the Hero Twins. Below, in the centre of the shell, is a skull with a sacrificial wristlet and a bouquet of coils. From the ends of the carapace emerge a toad on the left and the Patron of the Month Pax on the right. Attending the reborn Hun Hunahpu are his sons, Hunahpu at the left, and Xbalanque, right, pouring the contents of a large vessel over the carapace. Beneath the carapace appear waterlilies, symbols of rebirth and transformation, and the layered water-symbol. At a deep level, these represent the primeval ocean, the source of all life. (Drawings after incised bones from Temple I, Tikal, Guatemala, Late Classic Period, AD 735. Cyclindrical vessels, photo rollouts, Late Classic Period, AD 600–900. Tripod plate, Late Classic Period)

The Ballgame of the Gods

One of the chief trials in the confrontation between the Hero Twins and the Lords of Xibalba was the underworld ballgame. The exoteric aspects of this game, such as the layout and architecture of the ballcourts, *below*, found scattered through Mesoamerica, and the technical elements of the play are well known, though its full esoteric meaning and spiritual symbolism are less certain.

The ballgame was a dangerous sport that required skilful manipulation of a heavy rubber ball about a foot in diameter. The players wore protective garments on their legs and arms, *right*, the parts of the body that took most of the painful blows, and draped cloth beneath their yokes.

One to four players on either side competed in controlling the ball without touching it with their hands, and directing it toward markers or rings.

The objective was to make the ball pass through the ring, or at least to hit the marker. To drive the ball through the ring was very difficult; even the legendary players succeeded only a few times during their lives. Losers were sacrificed, *left*, and their hearts were offered to the sun god. Sometimes their severed heads were placed in play.

A relief carving from the Great Ballroom at Chichen Itza, *below*, depicts the culmination of the ballgame: the victorious player has decapitated the defeated with a sacrificial knife. The ball is represented between them as a belching skull. Six snakes and an elaborate tree sprouting from the loser's neck symbolize the fertility and life-energy this sacrifice will bring.

The deeper symbolism of the ballgame suggests that the player, like the Hero Twins who in the *Popol Vuh* defeated the Lords of Xibalba, has the capacity to triumph over death and gain rebirth. In the game played on a royal level, the Maya rulers may have dressed as the Hero Twins, thus enacting the roles of the demigods they emulated.

A scene carved on a tablet from Palenque carries a similar message of hope. The ruler's son in the guise of the underworld Jaguar God, with the sun sign in his headdress, dances out of a watery Xibalba to be greeted by his mother, who hands him a little figure of underworld God K, and welcomes him to the ranks of triumphant ancestors. (Ballplayer ceramic, Late Classic Period, AD 700–900. Ballcourt, Xochicalco. Relief, Sta Lucia Cotzumahualpa, Guatemala, c. AD 1000. Drawing after a relief at Chichen Itza, Mexico, Postclassic Period, AD 900–1200. Drawing after a relief from Temple 14, Palenque, Chiapas, Late Classic Period, AD 705)

Quetzalcoatl and the Redemption of Spirit from Matter

By far the most important archetypal symbol of death and rebirth in the Precolumbian world was Quetzalcoatl, a complex and multifaceted deity who could be represented in many different ways. He appears most frequently in the form of a plumed serpent, symbolizing the union of the earthly and spiritual elements, as he is shown, *left*, on a side of the pyramid of Xochicalco.

Quetzalcoatl's mother was the earth goddess, Coatlicue. When the Sun took her for his bride, all the generative and destructive forces of nature came into being, and Quetzalcoatl was the fruit of their union.

The giant sculpture of Coatlicue, *below left*, shows her dual head formed from two facing rattlesnakes and her skirt composed of writhing serpents. Her neck is shaped like a sacrificial vase, with a necklace of severed hands, hearts, and a skull. In her massive legs are the underworlds, the nine Aztec hells, and her heads contain the thirteen heavens. This seemingly monstrous figure was for the Aztecs a powerful reminder of the awesome forces of Mother Earth, to whom they owed their life and sustenance.

The Sun as the male generative power, Coatlicue as Earth, and Quetzalcoatl, associated with the planet Venus, formed a trinity in which harmony and balance were attained. While Coatlicue embodies primarily the forces that entrap the spirit in the material world, Quetzalcoatl symbolizes the possibility of redeeming matter and reconnecting it with spirit. The mysterious process through which this is possible is described in the myth of Quetzalcoatl's fall and penance (p. 21), embodying a profound experience of annihilation, transformation, and rebirth.

In another of his aspects, Quetzalcoatl appears as Ehecatl, god of wind, when he wears a bird-like mask. His association with death and rebirth (as breath of life) and reconciling function is suggested by a painting (*facing top*) showing him joined back-to-back with the skeletal god of death, Mictlantecuhtli.

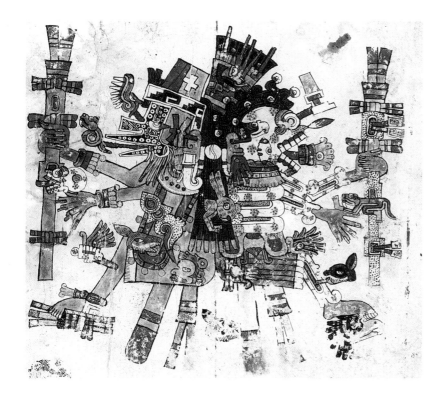

The story of Quetzalcoatl's journey through the underworld and transformation is told in the Codex Borgia, a Nahuatl screenfold filled with religious and ritualistic symbolism. In the East, the Place of Burning, Quetzalcoatl climbs on the pyre and is burned to death. His ashes are scattered by the wind and transformed into a flock of birds. His heart or spiritual essence does not die but rises from his ashes. Next he enters the South, the Place of Thorns, characterized by dismembering and decapitating (p. 88). In the West he passes two temples, one the abode of women who died in childbirth and the other of dead warriors. There Quetzalcoatl disappears into the maw of the Earth Dragon Cipactli, and emerges in two forms, the red and the black.

Quetzalcoatl is shown in the West as god of wind, *centre left*, opposite the god of the planet Venus, Tlahuizcalpantecuhtli, seated on a temple-platform. The open jaws of the Earth Dragon Cipactli support the platform. From skulls at either side flow two rivers, together forming the glyph for war. In the centre is a sacrificed captive, and above, a broken blood serpent and a sacrificial rope.

A further image from the Codex Borgia, *bottom left*, shows Quetzalcoatl's transformation inside a square representing the body of the goddess of death, and the dark centre of the subterranean kingdom. An urn shaped as a stylized skull holds his ashes, from which emerge serpentine banners symbolizing death, some bearing small heads of Quetzalcoatl as god of wind. Above the urn, the mortuary form of Quetzalcoatl arises, with the features of the deity of the Morning Star.

In the North, the darkest and lowest region, the red Quetzalcoatl is sacrificed by the black, and the black immolates himself. Transformed first into a hummingbird, he rises in the eastern sky as Venus, the Morning Star, Lord of Dawn. (Pyramid of Xochicalco, Mexico. Statue of Coatlicue, Late Postclassic Period, 1200–1519. Illustrations of the Codex Borgia, 15th century)

A main objective of the medieval *Ars moriendi* literature was to bring home the futility of a life-strategy dominated by the pursuit of external goals, such as wealth, possessions, power and fame. In their efforts to divert people from worldly ambitions and turn them toward God, the artists of *Ars moriendi* used the themes of death and impermanence.

Popular *memento mori* were Death's horseman, *above*, and the story of the 'Three living and three dead', *below*. This described how three young noblemen, when out hunting, came upon three corpses who either spoke or displayed their terrible warnings: 'Thus will ye be, and as ye are, so once were we'; 'Rich and poor alike must die', and, 'None shall escape death'. Here the message is displayed beside the coffins of three plague victims.

The dance of death, or *danse macabre*, was an extraordinary mass phenomenon that developed in France in the late thirteenth century and spread to the other countries of Europe. Its earliest known illustration was a series of paintings formerly in the cemetery of Les Innocents in Paris which showed the whole hierarchy of Church and State dancing with skeletons or corpses who escorted them to their graves. Although this graphic warning was destroyed in 1669, the explanatory verses survive, and a series of woodcuts published by the Paris printer Guy Marchant preserves the imagery. *Right*, from the top: death conducts a chambermaid and a matron, a doctor and a lover, a bride and a prostitute, an astrologer and a bourgeois, a pope and an emperor. (Woodcut from *Le grant kalendier* printed by Nicolas le Rouge, Troyes, 1496. Woodcuts from *La danse macabre des femmes*, 1486, and *La danse macabre des hommes*, 1485)

A second purpose of the *Ars moriendi* texts was to assist those on the point of death. Besides model prayers to Christ, Mary, and the Archangel Michael, and standard admonitions, there were other passages which advised on experiential aspects of dying. The phenomena usually referred to as 'attacks of Satan' were specific challenges which the dying typically experienced during the non-ordinary states of consciousness that occurred in their last hours. The Church interpreted these difficult experiences as resulting from the devil's desperate attempts to divert the souls from their way to Heaven at this critical time.

The 'attacks' fell under the headings of serious doubts regarding faith; desperation and agonizing qualms of con-

science; impatience and irritability due to suffering; conceit, vanity and pride; and greed, avarice, and other worldly concerns and attachments. Devils seize the miser's moneybags, *left*, and a dying man violently overturns a table.

These attempts of the devil were counteracted by divine interventions and influences that gave the dying a foretaste of Heaven, a sense of being subjected to Divine Judgment, a feeling of obtaining higher help, and a joyful promise of redemption. Many similar experiential sequences have been described in modern studies of death and dying. (*Death and the Miser*, by Hieronymous Bosch, c. 1450–1516. Woodcut from a German *Ars moriendi*, 15th century. Christ in Judgment, from Hartmann Schedel, *Weltchronik*, 1493)

Both the pedestal and body of the statue of the Aztec Xochipilli, Lord of Flowers, shown seated in ecstasy (*above*), are decorated with floral glyphs. These have been identified as stylized psychedelic plants: the caps of the sacred mushroom (Psilocybe aztecorum), morning glory flowers and tendrils, and hallucinogenic tobacco flowers. There is strong evidence that Precolumbian cultures gained their knowledge of the experiental territory of death, not only from accounts of near-death experiences, but from visionary states induced by a variety of psychedelic plants.

In the Highland Maya culture area of Guatemala, and in southern Mexico and El Salvator, archaeologists have long been uncovering mysterious stone figures with an umbrella-like top, mostly about a foot high and dated between 1000 BC and AD 500. In the last few decades research has identified these as effigies of psychedelic mushrooms. A ceramic from Colima in Mexico, *above right*, shows celebrants dancing around a mushroom-effigy which may also represent the World Tree, the *axis mundi*. Similar mushrooms can be found among the illustrations of Pre-

columbian codices. A leaf of an Aztec codex dating from the years immediately after the Conquest shows a celebrant eating sacred mushrooms, attended by the god of death, Mictlantecuhtli. Ritual use of the magic mushroom, known as *teonanacatl* or the 'flesh of the gods', is still common in contemporary Mexico, particularly among the Mazatec, Zapotec and Mixtec Indians.

Ritual use of the Mexican cactus peyote also dates back more than three thousand years, and continues in modern Mexico and among various tribes of North America. Paintings on vessels suggest that peyote was administered among the ancient Maya in the form of ritual enemas.

Modern psychopharmacology has been able to isolate and identify the active alkaloids from most psychedelic plants, and produce new psychedelic substances, like LSD. This has made it possible to conduct laboratory research into the visionary states induced by psychedelics. Two paintings illustrate a rebirth experience from a high-dose LSD session, *top, far right*. The first shows a terrifying archetypal figure obstructing the way to light, the

second portrays the ecstatic release, after the subject experienced annihilation by this figure.

Bloodletting was another powerful mind-altering method that opened up experiental realms not normally accessible until the time of biological death. Particularly among the Maya, bloodletting from the tongue, earlobe or penis was conducted on many occasions – when buildings were dedicated, crops planted, couples married, the dead buried, or wars initiated, and particularly at the completion of the twenty-year cycle, the *katun*. A Maya tablet (*right*) shows a priest piercing his tongue as an act of ritual self-sacrifice.

For kings, every event of political or religious importance required santification through bloodletting. A Maya lintel depicts Lady Xoc, the wife of the king Shield Jaguar, in a trance state as she draws a spiny rope through her tongue. (Statue, Mexico, Late Classic Period, AD 600–900. Terracotta figures from Colima, Mexico, 200 BC–AD 100. Leaf from the Codex Magliabecchi, Mexico. Contemporary psychedelic paintings. Relief, Mexico, Late Classic Period. Lintel from Yaxchilan, Chiapas, Mexico, Late Classic Period, AD 725)

Attitudes to the Human Body

The Books of the Dead differed considerably in the roles they ascribed the physical body, and in how they approached its mortality. Many passages of the *Pert em hru* attest to the ancient Egyptians' belief that the physical body was important for the afterlife. Meticulous care was devoted to the procedures of mummification, a complex process that took many weeks to complete. The brain was removed through nostils, and the liver, lungs, stomach and intestines were taken out of the body and placed in four canopic jars, or four compartments of a canopic chest, each under the protection of one of the four sons of Horus and linked to the cardinal points. The body cavities were filled with spices, resins, bitumen, or balls of linen, and the body was preserved in precious oils and resin, then wrapped in linen bandages together with magic ornaments and amulets.

All the materials used in embalming were considered the transformed tears shed by the gods at the death of Osiris, and conferred the powers of the gods on the deceased. Osiris's son Anubis, *top*, was in charge of ceremony, which ensured the rebirth of the deceased by re-enacting the events that raised Osiris from the dead.

At the tomb, a priest wearing the mask of Anubis conducted the 'Opening of the Mouth' ceremony (*right*) in accordance with the Book of the Dead (Chapter 23), to restore the ability to see, hear, eat and speak. Mythically this corresponded to the occasion when the god Horus visited his dead father Osiris after vanquishing his enemy Seth, and gave him his own eye which had been snatched by Seth during their battle, and so re-awakened him to consciousness.

In the pre-Conquest cultures of Central America the most striking practice involving the body was that of human sacrifice and self-sacrifice, sometimes premedicated with sacred mushrooms or peyote. In an Aztec ceremony, *bottom left*, the victim's heart is offered up to the sun god. The importance of death in the universal scheme was fully acknowledged and accepted, and human agents assumed control over its timing.

In the Christian tradition, while the flesh might be re-assumed at the time of universal judgment, the corruptibility of the body as bearer of sin was contrasted with the everlasting life of the spirit. A medieval tomb-sculpture, *above*, invites contemplation of the physical intimacy with worms and toads that death may bring.

The iconography of the *Bardo Thödol* abounds in human skulls, severed heads and hands and plucked-out eyes. However, these do not have a literal, but a deeply symbolic meaning. A specific type of painting for meditation represents a charnel field, as indicated by the upper border of hides, intestines and plucked-out eyes. It is intended to be completed mentally by the viewer, for often only the atttributes of the deities are shown. The primary concern of Tibetan ritual art in relation to death is to train the human mind to face the non-ordinary states of consciousness associated with the process of dying. During the bardo states the body is returned to the elements of which it is composed. (Papyrus of the Book of the Dead, showing embalmment. Papyrus of Hunefer, 19th Dynasty, c. 1310 BC. Drawing after the Aztec Codex Florentino. Tomb of François de la Sarra, La Sarraz, Vaud, c. 1400. Tanka painting, 19th century)

The Scenery and Inhabitants of the Netherworld

The scenery and inhabitants of the underworld described in the Books of the Dead vary in detail, but show ma[ny] similarities. The chthonic realms are dark, dismal, and ominous; they are places of dangers, ordeals and cruel punishment. While the hells of the Tibetan Book of the Dead and the Egyptian and Precolumbian underworlds were places through which the deceased or initiate could pass during their spiritual journey, the Christian Hell was the final destination, from which there was no escape.

The Maya name for the underworl[d] Xibalba, means 'place of fright': it had [a] plethora of terrifying deities, often

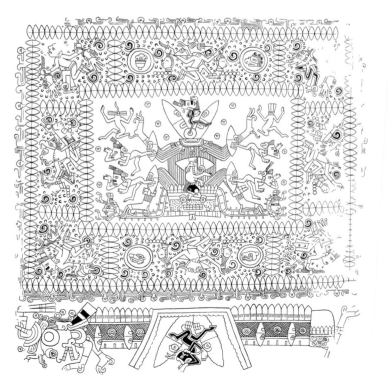

shown with aged, toothless human faces. The ruler God L is depicted, *far left*, seated on a jaguar throne supported by vertebrae and facing six young gods. Other gods are represented with distended bellies and wearing disembodied eyes and bones as jewelry, like two on the left of a detail from a funerary vase, *centre left*. Death God A is portrayed, *centre*, as almost toothless and holding a human skull.

The Aztec underworld included, at the South, the Place of Thorns (*far left, below*), a region characterized by cutting, piercing and decapitation. Here the goddess of voluptuousness, earth and death is shown sitting in a vessel shaped like a stylized skull. The figure of Quetzalcoatl appears between the goddess's head flints, emerges again from her chest flint, and having passed safely through this region, is shown below, continuing his perilous journey. The North, the darkest region of the Aztec hell, is ruled by Mictlantecuhtli, God of Death (*facing, bottom right*).

Christian mythology, like the Tibetan, describes hell as a place of demonic tormentors, consuming fire, crushing pressure, cutting and piercing: such tortures as are depicted in this detail of a medieval hell-scene (*left*).

The Egyptian underworld also had places of fire and devouring monsters. The final peril before dawn was the serpent Aapep, who barred the sun god's way until he was destroyed by the cat, Bastet (*left, below*). The Egyptian scene has a striking modern parallel in a painting from an LSD session in which the subject experienced death and rebirth (*left*). A sprouting seed and a foetus, symbolizing new life, are threatened by a giant snake, here representing the old, neurotic elements of the personality: guilt, aggression and fear. (Facing page: Drawing after the Vase of the Seven Gods, Late Classic Period, AD 600–900. Pottery figure, Tikal, Guatemala, AD 400–500. Drawing after a funeral vase, North Petén, Mexico, Late Classic Period. Drawing after the Codex Borgia, 15th century. Figure from Central Veracruz, Late Classic Period. This page: Detail of The Last Judgment, by Stephen Lochner, after 1440. Painting from the tomb of Inkheska, 16th–14th century BC. Contemporary psychedelic painting)

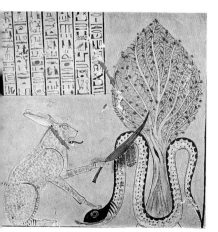

Animals of the Beyond

The pantheons of the Egyptian, Pre-columbian and Tibetan mythologies abound in animal symbolism. A wide variety of deities and their helpers or adversaries appear either in animal form, or as human figures with animal heads. Some of them are inhabitants of the underworlds, others belong to the celestial or paradisean realms. In some instances, states of psychospiritual transformation are expressed through the symbolism of animals and various aspects of nature. Typical are the Christian fish, lamb and peacock, the theriomorphic deities of the Egyptian and Tibetan pantheons, and the strange fauna of the Maya and Aztec underworlds.

A vase depicts animals of the Maya chthonic menagerie, *above left*. From the left, a Jaguar Dog is followed by a toad-like Uinal monster, holding an offering bowl containing an eye, a severed hand and long-bone. A fish nibbles at his waterlily headdress. Next follows a spider monkey with deer ears and a small bundle attached to its tail.

The Aztec god of death, Mictlante-cuhtli, is shown, *above right*, with the bird of the dead, an owl with a human skull for a head. It perches on a bundle of wood in a sacrificial offering bowl.

The Bat God, *right*, was the sharp-toothed adversary of the Hero Twins of the *Popol Vuh*, one of whom it managed to decapitate.

Subjects undergoing psychedelic therapy report encounters with terrifying animals as part of the process of psychological death and rebirth. Paintings from high-dose LSD sessions show, *left*, the foetus in the jaws of a snake, and threatened by a giant spider representing a devouring mother goddess, and, *right*, the pains of the uterine contractions experienced as attacks by giant predatory birds, yet accompanied by the promise of liberation, redemption, and rebirth.

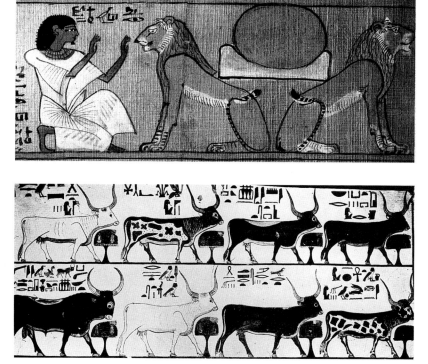

In Arabian mythology the phoenix had a life-span of five hundred years. Then the bird built a nest and laid an egg. The parent bird was burnt by the fire of the nest, ignited by the sun, and the heat of the same fire hatched the new phoenix. Here (*top left*) the deceased appears with the Egyptian version of the phoenix, the Bennu bird, illustrating the spell in the Book of the Dead (Chapter 13) which calls for the deceased to 'go forth as a phoenix' – that is, to be reborn.

The god Thoth, the divine scribe and Measurer of Time, was sometimes represented as a baboon. He is seen, *above left*, holding the Eye of Ra and wearing the lunar disc and crescent; the winged solar disc stresses his elevated position as defender of Ra.

In the Egyptian Book of the Dead, the deceased is identified with Osiris and often referred to by that name, while the reborn is identified with Ra and with the new day. Yesterday and Today (Osiris and Ra) were represented in a symbolic form as two lions. In this papyrus paint-

ing (*top right*) the deceased Hunefer is seen adoring the two lions; between them is the solar disc.

During their stay in the paradisean realms of the Egyptian Beyond, the blessed experienced great joy, and all their needs were satisfied. The divine nourishment and sustenance that they received there were symbolized by the seven celestial cows and a bull (*above*). The cat goddess Bastet (*left*) was the helper of the sun god. Her role in the solar barque was to kill Aapep, the giant serpent incarnation of Seth, archenemy of Osiris, and so assure the sun barque's emergence and the dawn of the new day. (Facing page: Vase of the Maya ceramic codex, Late Classic Period, AD 600–900. Detail from the Codex Borgia, 15th century. Bat, Zapotec sculpture. Contemporary psychedelic paintings. This page: Painting, tomb of Anhuskha, 20th Dynasty, 1200–1085 BC. Papyrus of Hunefer, 19th Dynasty, c. 1310 BC. Relief, 22nd Dynasty. Painting, tomb of Queen Nefertari, Thebes, c. 1250 BC. Bronze, Late Period, 664–332 BC)

Deities as Models

Every major culture of the world includes in its mythology archetypal figures representing death and rebirth, or transformation.

The texts of the Egyptian *Pert em hru* centre on two such figures: Ra, guiding the sun barque on the underworld voyage, and Osiris, killed, dismembered and resurrected, with whom the transfigured dead were identified. Those who successfully passed the Judgment were led to Osiris's kingdom (*above*). Here the deceased, the scribe Ani, kneels before Osiris in adoration, his own hair white like mummy-wrappings.

In preparing to face death and meet the perils and ordeals of the underworld, the ancient Maya had the example of the Hero Twins, whose resourcefulness enabled them to vanquish the Xibalba Lords, die by their own volition and return to youthful life. A scene of two Lords and a bat hovering overhead (*left*) recalls the Twins' ordeal in the House of the Bats, where Hunahpu was decapitated.

Precolumbian mythology had another powerful figure in Quetzalcoatl, who in penance for incest with his sister immolated himself, passed through the regions of the underworld and emerged as Venus, the Morning Star. In his life-giving aspect as the god of wind, *above right*, he dances in front of Tezcatlipoca, who symbolizes matter: a dualistic opposition of matter and spirit, each of which has something the other lacks and needs. A figure of Quetzalcoatl as Lord of Life reverses to Lord of Death (*above*), reflecting the dialectic of these two aspects of existence.

In the medieval monastic tradition the figure of Christ was explicitly used as a model for the spiritual path. In suffering and dying in meditation, monks practised *imitatio Christi*. According to Christian mythology, between the time of his death on the cross and resurrection (*right*) Jesus descended to Hell and liberated sinners from eternal damnation.

The victory over death found expression in several episodes from the Buddha's life. Here (*far right*) Kama Mara, Lord of Illusion, representing the forces of desire and fear of death, has made his last attempt to prevent the Buddha from reaching Enlightenment. He has sent his three daughters to divert him, and when this failed, attacked him with an army of demons. Sakyamuni Buddha is shown in deep meditation. The Buddha's victory comes when he dies, and enters paranirvana. (Facing page: Papyrus of Ani, 19th Dynasty, *c.* 1250 BC. Drawing after the Bloomington Vase, North Petén, Late Classic Period, AD 600–900. This page: Codex Borbonicus, 16th century. Statue, Huastec culture, Early Postclassic Period, AD 900–1250. Illuminated MS, 13th century. Tanka painting, *c.* 19th century)

Transcendence and the Emergence into Light

The posthumous adventures of the soul, as they are described in the ancient Books of the Dead, are full of challenges and ordeals, but they also offer many important promises. Thus the Egyptian and Precolumbian Books describe the possibility of overcoming all obstacles and experiencing rebirth, or attaining a joyful existence in various abodes of the blessed. The Christian literature promises those who have lived a good life and overcome all the temptations associated with dying, the eternal bliss of Heaven or Paradise, a realm of radiant, supernatural light. The Tibetan Book of the Dead also describes the possibility of rebirth into celestial and paradisean realms; however, the ultimate goal of Tibetan spiritual seekers is to achieve liberation from rebirth into any of the realms.

On a carved sarcophagus, *top left* the transition between the diurnal and nocturnal realms is symbolized as a transfer of the sun disc between two solar barques, one for the night journey, the other for the day. The deceased is shown twice, kneeling over each barque: this symbolizes the core of ancient Egyptian belief – that human life belongs to both the phases of eternity.

Modern psychological research has revealed that ecstatic experiences of spiritual rebirth, and of the paradisean and celestial realms, emerge spontaneously in non-ordinary states of consciousness. A painting from an LSD session, *left*, shows the foetus as a divine child sitting on a resplendent golden lotus, symbol of transcendence and rebirth. Another painting from a psychedelic session, *below left*, shows a deep connection between the oceanic ecstasy of an undisturbed intrauterine

state and the experience of a universe filled with the light of millions of stars.

In Dante's version of the Christian posthumous journey, the glorified souls dwell among the celestial spheres. *Above*, Dante and Beatrice leave the heaven of Venus and approach that of the sun.

The gold disc poised on the head of Ra as a falcon, *right*, shows the god in the form of Khepri, the scarab who rolled the ball of the sun nightly through the underworld toward the east. He is depicted here with the wings of Horus who carried the sun across the day sky, suggesting the image of the moment of dawn, and the rebirth of the soul. (Relief from the sarcophagus of Djed-hor, c. 6th century BC. Contemporary psychedelic paintings Illumination by Giovanni di Paolo for the *Paradiso* of Dante's *Divine Comedy*, c. 1445. Carving from Tutankhamen's chariot, 1357–49 BC)

BIBLIOGRAPHY

Arnold, P., *Das Totenbuch der Maya*, Scherz Verlag, Bern, 1980.

Andrews, C., *The Ancient Egyptian Book of the Dead*, Macmillan Publishing Company, New York City, 1985.

Bilder und Tanze des Todes: Gestalten des Todes in der europaeischen Kunst seit dem Mittelalter. Eine Ausstellung des Kreises Unna (Exhibition catalogue), 1982.

Budge, W.E.A., *Osiris: the Egyptian Religion of Resurrection*. University Books, New Hyde Park, NY, 1961.

Budge, W.E.A., *The Book of the Dead*, University Books, New Hyde Park, NY 1964.

Cavendish, R., *Visions of Heaven and Hell*, Harmony Books, New York City, 1977.

Champdor, A., *The Book of the Dead: From the Ani, Hunefer, and Anhai Papyri in the British Museum*. Garrett Publications, New York City, 1966.

Codice Borgia, Fondo de cultura economica, Mexico City, 1980.

Coe, M.D., *Lords of the Underworld: Masterpieces of Classic Maya Ceramics*, The Art Museum, Princeton University, Princeton, NJ., 1978, distributed by Princeton University Press.

Delacour, J.B., *Glimpses of the Beyond*, Harwood Smart, London, 1975.

Douce, F., *The Dance of Death*, William Pickering, London, 1983.

Eberhard, O., *Egyptian Art and the Cults of Osiris and Amon*, Thames and Hudson, London, 1968.

Eichenberg, F., *Dance of Death: A Graphic Commentary on the Danse Macabre Through the Centuries*, Abbeville Press, New York City, 1983.

Evans-Wentz, W.Y. (ed.), *The Tibetan Book of the Dead*, Oxford University Press, 1960.

Fremantle, F and C. Trungpa (ed. and trans): *The Tibetan Book of the Dead: The Great Liberation Through Hearing in the Bardo*, Shambhala Publications, Berkeley, CA, 1975.

Furst, P.T. and M.D. Coe, *Ritual Enemas*, Natural History, 86:88–91, 1977.

Grof, S., *The Human Encounter with Death*, E.P. Dutton, New York, 1967.

Hughes, R., *Heaven and Hell in Western Art*, Stein and Day Publishers, New York City, 1968.

Kuebler-Ross, E., *On Death and Dying*, Collier-Macmillan, London, 1969.

Lamy, L.: *Egyptian Mysteries: New Light on Ancient Knowledge*, Thames and Hudson, London, New York, 1981 (repr. 1991).

Lauf, I.D., *Secret Doctrines of the Tibetan Book of the Dead*, Shambhala Publications, Boulder, CO, 1977.

Mallakh, K. el, and R. Bianchi, *Treasures of the Nile*, Newsweek, New York, 1980.

Moody, R., *Life After Life*, Corgi Books, London, 1977.

Osis, K., et al., *Deathbed Observations of Physicians and Nurses*. Parapsychology Foundation, New York, 1961.

Rainer, R., *Ars Moriendi: Von der Kunst des heilsamen Lebens und Sterbens*, Boehlau Verlag, Koeln-Graz, 1957.

Ring, K., *Life at Death*, Coward, McCann & Geohegan, New York, 1980.

Ring, K., *Heading Toward Omega*, William Morrow & Co, New York, 1984.

Robicsek, F., *The Maya Book of the Dead: The Ceramic Codex*, Published by the University of Virginia Art Museum, Charlottesville, VA, 1981, distributed by the University of Oklahoma Press, Norman, Oklahoma.

Rossiter, E., *The Book of the Dead: Papyri of Ani, Hunefer, Anhai*. Miller Graphics, distributed by Crown Publishers.

Sabom, M., *Recollections of Death*, Simon & Schuster, New York, 1982.

Schele, L., and M.E. Miller, *The Blood of Kings*. George Braziller, Inc, New York, 1986, Thames and Hudson, London, 1992.

Weisse, J.E., *The Vestibule*, Ashley Books, Port Washington, NY.

SOURCES OF ILLUSTRATIONS

Courtesy of the author 29, 31, 52 *below*, 58 *top*, 89 *below right*, 90 *below left and right*, 94 *centre and below*; Amsterdam, Rijksmuseum-Stichting 38; Photo: Brian Beresford 74 *below*, 75 *top*; Berlin, Staatliche Museen Pesussischer Kulturbesitz 79 *left*; Photo: Edwin Bernbaum (1988) 70 *right*; Bologna, Pinacoteca (Photo Scala) 44; Boston, Gift of John Goelet. Courtesy, Museum of Fine Arts, Boston 42; Chantilly, Musée Condé 57; Courtesy Michael D. Coe 80 *top*, 88 *top left*; Cologne, Wallraf-Richartz Museum 89 *top*; Copenhagen, Ny Carlsberg Glyptothek 51, 67 *left*; Dallas Museum of Art. The Eugene and Margaret McDermott Fund, in honor of Mrs. Alex Spence 52 *top*; Robert Hatfield Ellsworth Private Collection (Photo John Bigelow Taylor, N.Y.C. 1991) 70 *left*; Werner Forman 55, 69 *below left*, 95 *below*; Photo Franceschi 54; Photo: Peter T. Furst 84 *top right*; Irmgard Groth 78 *below*; Photo André Held 86 *top*, 89 *below left*; Hirmer Fotoarchiv 60, 67 *right*, 68 *centre*, 91 *top left*; Andy Jillings 41; Justin Kerr 18 (© 1975), 52 *top* (© 1985), 69 *right* (© 1989), 76 *below* (© 1975), 77 *centre* (© 1975) and 77 *below* (© 1982), 78 *top* (© 1985), 90 *top left* (© 1980); Kodansha Ltd, Tokyo 56; La Sarraz Chapel, Vaud (Photo Gaston de Jongh) 87 *top*; Photo Dr Detlef I. Lauf 14, 15, 16, 73 *left*; London, British Library 93 *below left*, 95 *top*; Copyright British Museum 8, 47, 63 *below*, 64, 66 *centre*, 66 *below left and right*, 68 *top*, 85 *below right*, 86 *centre*, 91 *top right*, 91 *below*, 91 *centre left*, 92 *top*; By courtesy of the Board of Trustees of the Victoria and Albert Museum 39, 71 *below right*; Los Angeles County Museum of Art. From the Nasli and Alice Heeramaneck Collection. Museum Associates Purchase 71 *centre right*; The MacQuitty International Photographic Collection 48, 53, 68 *below*; Madrid, Museo del Prado (Photo Arxiu Mas) 36–37; Melbourne, reproduced by permission of The National Gallery of Victoria, Felton Bequest (1920) 62–63; Mexico City, Fondo Editorial de la Pastica 90 *centre*; Museo Nacional de Antropologia 65; Museo Nacional de Antropologia (photo Irmgard Groth) 19 *top*, 35, 65, 80 *below*, 84 *top left*, 85 *below left*, 88 *below right*; Munich, Staatliches Museum für Völkerkunde 87 *right*; Newark, Collection of The Newark Museum. Purchase 1969. The Members' Fund (Photo John Bigelow Taylor, N.Y.C. 1991) 45; New York, Courtesy of the Brooklyn Museum 69 *right* (Charles Edwin Wilbour Fund), 93 *top right* (Henry L. Batterman and Frank S. Benson Funds); The Metropolitan Museum of Art 43 (Fletcher Fund 1933), 69 *top*; Oxford, Ashmolean Museum 72 *left*; Paris, Bibliothèque de l'Assemblée Nationale 93 *top left*; Musée du Louvre (© Photo R.M.N.) 94 *top*; Musée Guimet (© Photo R.M.N.) 33; Philadelphia, courtesy University Museum (Photo W.R. Coe) 88 *top right*; Pisa, Camposanto (Photo Alinari) 34, 82 *below left*; Prague, Collection of Dr Milan Hausner 85 *top and centre right*; National Library 59; Courtesy Dr Francis Robiscek 19 *below* (From *The Smoking Gods* by Francis Robiscek), 63 *top* (From *The Book of the Dead. The Mayan Codex* by Francis Robiscek and Donald Hales); St Petersburg, The State Hermitage. Prince Ukhtomsky Collection (Photo John Bigelow Taylor N.Y.C. 1991) 71 *top right*; By courtesy of Linda Schele 76 *top*, 77 *top*, 79 *centre right and below right*; Strasbourg, Musée de l'Oeuvre Notre Dame (Photo Museés de la Ville) 40; Karl Taube 18, 20; Utica, Munson-Williams-Proctor Institute 78 *top*; Vatican, Biblioteca Apostolica 49, 81, 90 *top right*; Venice, Biblioteca Nazionale Marciana 50; Verona, Museo di Castelvecchio (Photo Scala) 61; Vienna, Kunsthistorisches Museum 46; Photo H. Roger Viollet (Collection Viollet) 91 *centre right*; Washington, The National Gallery of Art. Samuel H. Kress Collection (1952) 83 *top left*; The Zimmerman Family Collection (Photo John Bigelow Taylor N.Y.C. 1991) 72 *right*.